LOWERING YOUR
GOLF
HANDICAP

LOWERING YOUR
GOLF
HANDICAP

CHRIS MEADOWS
WITH
ALLEN F. RICHARDSON

This is a Parragon Book
This edition published in 2005

Copyright © Parragon 2001

Parragon
Queen Street House
4 Queen Street
Bath BA1 1HE
United Kingdom

Designed, produced and packaged by
Stonecastle Graphics Limited

Edited by Philip de Ste. Croix

ISBN 1-40544-616-1

Printed in China

Photography by Bill Johnston

Film kindly supplied by Fuji

I would like to thank The Wisley Golf Club,
Surrey, England and Le Prince de Provence,
Vidauban, France for allowing me the use of
their wonderful golfing facilities. They are
truly two of the finest golf courses to be
found anywhere in Europe.

Thanks also go to my professional colleague
Daniel Belcher, Nicola Bustin, my wife
Kayo, to the two men who worked so
closely with me in over a year of preparation,
Allen Richardson and Bill Johnston, but
most of all to my teacher Ian Connelly who
developed my love for golf and gave me the
passion to teach this great game.

CONTENTS

◆◆◆◆◆

A VOYAGE OF DISCOVERY

◆◆◆◆◆

CHRIS MEADOWS' love of the game began at the age of 12. While caddying at a golf club in North London, he was introduced to a Scottish professional, Ian Connelly. In the mid 1970s Connelly was coaching the cream of European talent including his star pupil Nick Faldo. Meadows, himself aspiring to become a successful tour player, found himself intrigued by the array of skills Connelly possessed and the way he developed players' minds and movements, often taking them from nothing to scratch golfers. By the age of 16 Chris knew that he had begun a voyage of discovery that would last a lifetime.

Over an eight-year period working with Connelly as both pupil and teacher, Meadows spent literally thousands of hours watching players of all standards being taught by Connelly on practice grounds across Europe. By now he'd begun using his own game as a testbed, seeking to understand the perfect motion. His golf was improving to a high standard, but he found that his own stable of players were demanding more and more of his time.

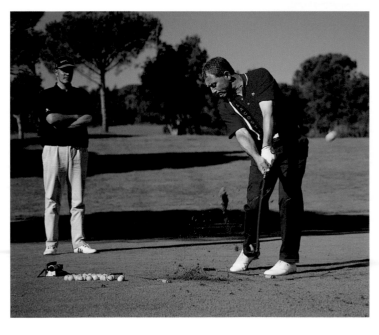

THE RIGHT ENVIRONMENT

Although commanding his own head pro position by the age of 21, increasingly Meadows became frustrated with the generally poor teaching conditions in the UK. He vowed to develop his own school of excellence where golfers of all standards could be stimulated by their environment, as well as by their teacher. In 1987 Meadows acquired The Regent's Park Golf & Tennis School in the heart of Central London. Driven by the belief that seeing is believing, he installed the most advanced video systems of the time so that students of the school could understand and see for themselves their own swing in action. The school soon became an outstanding success

Left: A stimulating environment is an essential part of learning. Meadows designs all his golf schools with a strong emphasis on visual learning. He says 'A picture is worth a thousand words and that's why video analysis and mirrors are so useful to both pupil and teacher'.

and Meadows was invited to write instructional columns for numerous golf publications. He developed the concept for *Improve your Golf* (a golf learning manual) that was published in the UK, Australasia, Canada and even translated into Japanese selling over 500,000 copies in total. He has written five instructional golf books, appeared on BBC, Channel 4, Channel 5 and many satellite channels and has made four instructional videos.

In 1997 Meadows opened the first Metro Golf Centre in London. These are centres of golfing excellence incorporating everything a golfer might ever need to advance their game. Based on a golf-for-all philosophy, the centre has become the industry standard for golf centres in Europe.

Above: If it's fun, you'll keep at it – enjoy your 'voyage of discovery'.

www.chrismeadowsgolf.com

Meadows has always used his entrepreneurial skills to take the game to the people and he has recently launched an interactive website 'www.chrismeadowsgolf.com'. The site is a very different experience in learning. Driven once again by visual aids, simplicity and structure (the trademark of Meadows teaching), it helps players plan their improvement and effectively guides them to their chosen objective.

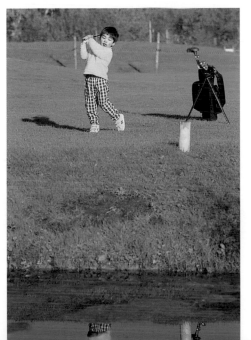

Left: If your children want to play the game, put them in a group class first – they'll have fun and meet friends with whom they can play.

INTRODUCTION

◆ ◆ ◆ ◆ ◆

Golfers are dreamers and seekers.
From the first time we pick up a club and hit that small, round object
known as a golf ball towards the sky, we are part of a tradition that
stretches back through generations of time, linking us to an ancient
shepherd who first struck a rock with a stick along the coastal grassland
of Scotland.

FROM THAT moment we often embark on a life-long quest to improve how we play the game – a game that for most of us eventually becomes both a love and an obsession. From tour pro to club champion to rank beginner, we constantly tinker with our swings, adjust our grips and stances, and try to plant an endless series of 'swing thoughts' in our brains.

The hope is that by tomorrow, next weekend – or at least the end of the year – we will finally play a miracle round.

GOLFING DREAMS

The form that round takes will vary. We might dream of breaking 100 or 70, sinking an eagle putt, winning the club championship, or standing on the 18th tee with a chance to seize the Open. But at the very least, we all yearn for the day when we'll win that side bet struck with our similarly devoted friends, while savouring a drink at the 19th hole. Then we'll enjoy the afterglow of a memorable day, with everyone mentally replaying their rounds, and generously

The hours spent working on my game have been some of the most enjoyable of my life. I hope this book also makes learning fun for you in your quest to improve your game.

reviewing each other's remembered highlights.

But even when we are not playing the game, we take lessons, analyze how more gifted players perform on television and read countless articles about the the latest technology in club design, swing theory and putting technique.

I know. I've spent a lifetime playing, teaching and trying to improve my own game – and this book is the product of my quest, while your purchase of it is undoubtedly proof that you share my passion.

Lowering Your Golf Handicap is written for the player who understands the basics of the game and possesses a reasonably consistent technique. This book explores the many situations which you are bound to encounter almost every time you play. But we begin with the only factor outside of yourself that can really influence the way you play – your golf equipment. There can be little doubt that there are few games or sports where products are hyped as much as they are in golf, so we look at just what is important when selecting your equipment and the effect it can have on your game.

Now you are properly equipped, you've developed the perfect swing on the driving range and you are able to hit the ball quite consistently. But, as any experienced golfer will explain, disaster is often lurking just around the corner. What separates a fine golfer from an average golfer is how he or she can deal with difficult situations. If you need proof of that just watch Tiger Woods play any round of golf; he has a huge repertoire of shots at his disposal for every circumstance. You will find the need for plenty of these shots during most rounds that you play, so I have included a section entitled 'Advanced Ball Control'. Knowing how to hit the ball high or low, to move it right or left, will give you confidence to play in any conditions.

A good lie on the fairway is a great advantage but what if your ball ends up in a divot? In 'Mastering Awkward Lies' I look at

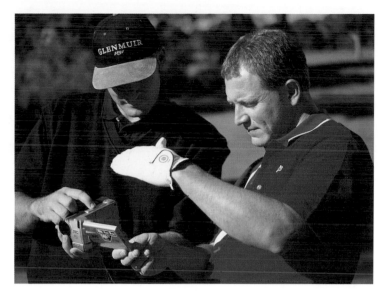

almost every eventuality. But what if your technique suddenly deserts you? Golf is a fickle game and it seems all too often that just before that crucial competition you develop a slice, hook, or even the dreaded shank for seemingly no reason. Don't panic, because help is at hand in 'Faults and Cures'. This section explores the majority of common golfing maladies and offers some instant remedies to get you back on track. I conclude with a section on that ultimate shot saver, 'Putting'. Anybody can be a good putter – all you need is a little expert instruction.

Over the years I have had the opportunity to work with some great teachers who have shared their knowledge with me. It is now my privilege to share my knowledge with you.

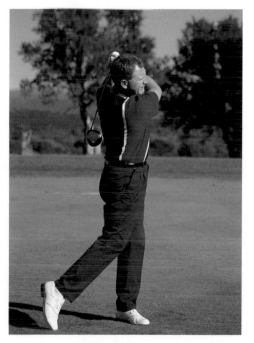

The great thing about golf is we are always learning. When man has mastered the wildest dreams of future technology, he will still be working on his golf swing!

EQUIPMENT

◆ ◆ ◆ ◆ ◆

Purchasing golf equipment is like choosing a pair of shoes for a child. If they do not fit correctly, they will be uncomfortable and have undesirable long-term consequences.

SELECTING YOUR EQUIPMENT

◆ ◆ ◆ ◆ ◆

No two men or women are exactly the same, and none of us swings a golf club in an identical fashion. Our height, arm length, hand size, strength, tempo, swing speed and the shape of our average shot – whether relatively straight, a fade or a draw – inevitably differ to some extent.

A S A RESULT, when choosing clubs, you should consider at least four key factors: the swingweight, lie angle (the angle between the sole of the club and the shaft when the club is held with the clubhead flat on the ground), type of shaft, and the size – or thickness – of the grips. The length, weight and flex of club shafts can make a profound difference to your performance, as does grip thickness and the type of clubhead used. Stainless steel, mild steel, graphite and titanium heads are each better suited to some golfers than others.

In golf, like in love, one man's meat is another's poison.

RIGHT FOR YOUR GAME

The same holds true for golf balls. Selecting the right one for your game, and the weather conditions in your area, can make a big difference to your score. Even the right golf shoe can profoundly affect performance. Balance, the key to any good golf swing, starts from the spikes up.

Staying dry and comfortable over long rounds is also a contributing factor to performing well, so purchasing the correct clothing is essential to playing good golf.

Even the type of golf bag you pick can make a difference. If you have to carry your own bag, weight becomes a major consideration. And depending on the

Above: Even the choice of a golf bag needs to be thought about. They come in all shapes and sizes.

Left: The pro shop is an Aladdin's Cave for most golfers. But if you're choosing golf clubs, make sure you can hit the ball with trial clubs on the range before making any decision.

weather conditions prevalent where you play, the number and depth of the pockets is important for storing wet-weather gear and/or warm clothing.

CUSTOMIZED GOLF CLUBS

Let's first consider clubs. Unless you know your own swing well, and have played the game in various situations and conditions, you may not feel comfortable enough – nor be knowledgeable enough – to select your own equipment from the vast amount available at retail.

Even if you do, I would suggest grilling the salesperson to see if they know enough about the clubs that they are touting and can assure you that they will fit your game – or *can* be fitted to your game.

But here's a better approach. If you are not already taking lessons from a qualified PGA (Professional Golfers Association) professional, find one. Now!

VESTED INTEREST

A pro can assess your swing and level of skill, then recommend a set of clubs that is right for you. Such a pro will also have a vested interest in your improvement – you may want to remain a team during the lifetime journey that golf can become. Consequently, the pro can generally be relied upon to give you good advice.

Ask for a variety of demonstration models – which most pros are happy to lend to prospective buyers – before buying any new club. The pro can watch you practise your swing and give you further advice on which particular club might suit your game, while you decide if you like the look and feel of the clubs.

Now you're finally ready to buy.

Again, you can pay good money for what's available off the shelf, or you can be smart. Increasingly, large manufacturers such as Ping, Titleist, Zevo and Dynacraft, to name only a few, build custom-made golf clubs at competitive prices. Ask your pro for a recommendation, and have some simple measurements taken so that a 'fitted' set can

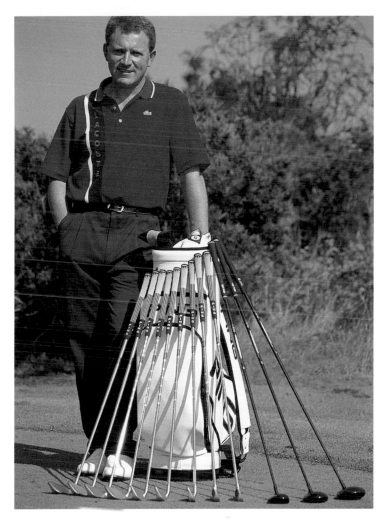

be designed and made to suit your specific physique and swing.

Some manufacturers even offer components that can be temporarily assembled into demonstration clubs, building a variety of sample clubs you can test on a range until you feel comfortable and the pro is satisfied you have the proper fit – from driver to wedge.

Your new clubs will help you to develop the proper posture, grip and swing, the key to playing better golf and a lifetime of fun.

The conventional set of golf clubs is normally made up of nine irons, three woods, a putter and maybe a utility wedge or wood, totalling fourteen.

Even two-year-olds are well served these days.

THE CLUBHEAD

◆ ◆ ◆ ◆ ◆

Modern science and even the space programme have contributed greatly to the variety of materials now used in clubheads – the only part of the club that comes into contact with the ball – and the way they are built. Once only made of wood, cast or forged steel, clubhead design and construction is now a highly sophisticated art using high-tech materials, and one from which your game can greatly benefit.

IRONS HAVE either bladed or peripherally weighted heads. The traditional bladed head is still often seen in the bag of the tour professional – check out what your favourite pro uses the next time you watch a tournament on television – or the low handicap player who can hit most of his or her shots in the centre of the clubface.

But increasingly, the more modern peripherally weighted golf club – which came into general use about 20 years ago and which has an oversized clubhead with a cavity back – is replacing the bladed club. Originally designed to help beginners and golfers who do not possess a consistent swing and who are thus more liable to mis-hit shots, peripherally weighted clubs now find favour with such top pros such as Tiger Woods, Colin Montgomerie and David Duval.

INCREASED SWEET SPOT

With the weight distributed around the outside of the head, these clubs are more forgiving, much like larger tennis rackets which offer an increased sweet spot. Even when a shot is hit off-centre, the result is often a fairly reasonable strike.

As for woods, the clubheads these days are made of anything but wood, featuring such materials as steel, graphite and titanium. Metal woods – rather than the traditional wooden ones that dominated the game for decades – are now used by players at every level.

The clubheads are hollow and peripherally weighted, making them easier to hit and easier to maintain. Plus, they wear well.

As to the swingweight of the clubhead, that is an individual choice. A golfer should try out as large a variety of swingweights as

Lie angle can be adjusted on most irons and on some woods (often only when manufactured). If you want to test your clubs, make a straight line on the ball with a pen, place the line at right angles to the ground and hit the ball. If the club fits, the line will be transferred straight down the clubface.

Marking the ball to determine the lie angle of a wood

Checking and adjusting dynamic lie angle

possible to determine which one suits him or her best. This is one area where there are no hard and fast rules.

DYNAMIC LIE

Lie angle is determined by the angle at which the shaft enters the head, and should be set by the manufacturer to suit a golfer's height, stature and arm length. But the only way really to determine the correct lie angle is by hitting shots. Merely holding a club to the ground, or taking up your address position with a club in a shop, will tell you almost nothing relevant about lie angle.

A number of factors have a direct bearing on the way the club returns to the ball at impact, so lie angle is an area where having clubs correctly fitted to you can make all the difference to your game. The wrong lie angle can lead to shots hit either left or right of the target, depending on whether the lie angle is too flat or too upright.

DETERMINING LIE ANGLE

To determine the correct lie angle for you, ask your pro to provide a number of clubs with different lie angles. The pro can then put some tape on the bottom of the clubs and let you hit shots off a hard board. The way the tape is rubbed off as you hit the ball will help him determine the right lie angle for you.

For example, if the tape gets worn at the toe, that means the club is too flat for you, and the ball could well shoot off to the right. Conversely, if the tape is worn at the heel, the club is too upright for you, and you may hit everything left.

Ideally, you're looking for a lie angle where the tape is rubbed off at the middle, indicating that the sole of the club is meeting the ground correctly at the moment of impact. That's called dynamic lie.

If your clubs do not have the right lie angle, it will have an adverse effect on how you hit the ball. The more lofted the club is, the more pronounced is the effect. Even 2 degrees off on a pitching wedge can be disastrous. So ensuring that your clubs have the right lie angle is yet another vital ingredient to playing that dream round.

Above and below: The dynamic lie angle of an iron can be measured either by the line method outlined for the wood, or by placing some tape on the bottom of your iron and hitting balls off a lie board (hard plastic). If the tape wears off the centre it's perfect – but if the wear is on the toe or heel end, get the club adjusted.

FLEX AND LENGTH OF SHAFTS

◆◆◆◆◆

Many golfers are of average height, strength and build compared with the rest of the population. Therefore, most store-bought clubs – which are manufactured to meet those averages – ought to suit them for flex and shaft length. At least in theory.

BUT CONSIDER this: if you're taller than some, shorter than others, nearing middle age, or unable to practise and play golf often enough to develop a consistent swing – more than once a week for both practice and playing – then you are not really average at all! In other words, although most of us are physically similar to our fellow men or women, we are not all the same when it comes to playing the game of golf. So you will want to give careful consideration to choosing the flex and length of your shafts.

THE RIGHT SHAFT

Shafts generally come in four very different flexes: L (ladies), A (quite flexible), R (regular mens) and S (stiff mens).

What's right for you? Obviously, L is meant for women golfers, though some stronger ladies would be advised to try the A or even R shafts to see if they suit them.

Alternatively, some men – especially as they age and lose some wrist and arm strength – feel more comfortable with the 'whippier' A shafts, rather than the traditional R or S.

Choosing the correct shaft for your game is so important. The shaft is literally the engine of the golf club; select the wrong one and it simply won't fire when required.

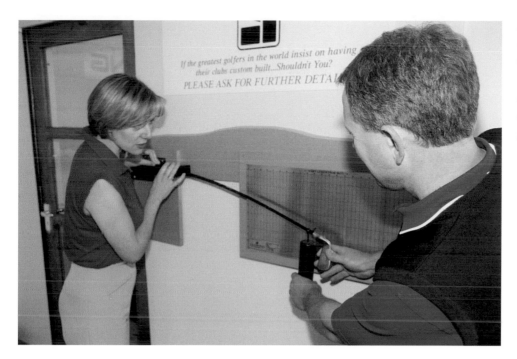

A set of clubs should be consistent in the way they flex. If you have a problem or a favourite club in a set, get it checked out – it may be different from the rest.

As for length, women's clubs have traditionally been built an inch (2.5cm) shorter than men's clubs when provided as standard manufactured sets. But again, with women's physiques changing through diet and more athletic training, it is best to have a pro measure you to establish the right length of shaft.

As a general rule, any man taller than 6 feet 2 inches (1.88m) needs a shaft that is a half to one inch (1.27 to 2.5cm) longer than standard, while men shorter than 5 feet 5 inches (1.65m) need a shorter length. For women shorter than 5 feet 2 inches (1.57m), the shorter length is best, while those over 5 feet 6 inches (1.68m) need longer shafts.

GRIP SIZE

Don't underestimate the importance of grip size, both for feel, comfort and its effect on shot-making. Grips that are too thick for a particular person's hands can actually result in a nasty slice or push (see definitions listed later in the glossary), while grips that are too thin can lead to pulled or hooked shots.

To check if a grip is the right size for you, place your left hand lightly on the grip, then close your fingers. Your two middle fingers should just touch the palm, or pad, of your hand.

Grips are made of leather, rubber or cord, though in recent years rubber has become the overwhelming choice for both standard clubs sold in stores and those fitted and built by a pro shop.

Keep your grips in good condition by regularly washing them with a mild soap and water solution, and have them replaced at least once a year by a qualified PGA professional clubmaker. The cost is minimal and the benefits enormous.

Grips come in different sizes, textures, patterns and much more. Try a few before deciding just which grip you would like fitted to your clubs.

CHOOSING A PUTTER

◆◆◆◆◆

*There are almost as many types of putter on the market as there are
golfers – which is quite appropriate. Putting is the most individual aspect
of the game and golfers approach this shot with a variety of pre-shot
routines, set-ups and grips. So it should not be surprising that the club
they use also varies to an enormous degree.*

PUTTERS CAN have shafts that are
extremely short or as long as a
broomstick. The blade can be flat
on both sides of the head, partially rounded
on one side like a mallet, heel-shafted,
centre-shafted or offset. Some sport a flange,
and many have an aiming line – or even two
– to assist in sizing up the target.

THE SHORTEST CLUB

But a few things are constant about putters
and how a golfer can use them. The putt is
the only shot in golf where the ball does not
travel at least partially through the air. The
idea is to roll the ball over the short grass on
the greens, although in some circumstances,
you can also putt through the longer grass
on the fringe of a green, from parts of the
fairway, or even across the sand in a bunker.

But because the ball remains in contact
with whatever surface you are trying to
cover, the putter is designed as the shortest

club in the bag (with the exception of the
long-shafted varieties favoured by a minority
of players), the most upright, and the one
with the least loft – between 2-4 degrees.
The head is small and thus meant only for
relatively short distances, and the grip –
although sometimes round like any other
club – is often flat at the front, to
accommodate the unique way a golfer holds
this club.

PUTTER CHARACTERISTICS

Putters come with three types of clubhead
positions: onset, offset and straight. Your
hands will be in front of the club face with
an offset putter, while the straight-headed
putter face will be level with your hands
when you line up. With an onset putter, your
hands will be behind the club face.

It's vital to try all three types of putter
before choosing the model that suits you,
based on how easy you find it to aim

Putters are often marked
on the grip with their
length.

There are an enormous
variety of putters. Soft
face, titanium face, Ping,
Zing, Wild Thing – the
list is endless. But before
you buy, just ask one
question – do I believe I
can get the ball in the
hole with this?

correctly. Obviously, taking the right aim is the most important way to sink putts consistently.

Many putters also have lines on the clubhead to help you aim accurately. These line markings should be set precisely at right angles to the face. Some are also intended to reveal the putter's sweetspot, which can be a tremendous help to the average golfer.

But be careful when considering bargain basement putters. I have come across several models where the markings were less than accurate, and that flaw could affect how many putts you make. Anything that interferes with successful putting is a huge detriment to your game, since nearly half your strokes will be taken on the green.

BALANCE AND SWINGWEIGHT

A putter with good balance and the proper swingweight for you is vital to executing a smooth putting stroke. Balance refers to the distribution of weight in the clubhead, while swingweight is the weight distribution along the length of the whole club.

You may have heard the term 'heel and toe', which refers to the most popular form of balance in putters. With this type of putter, most of the weight is concentrated in the two ends of the blade. The idea is to prevent the putter from twisting in your hands when the blade strikes the ball. If it does, the ball will go off line.

The swingweight of putters can vary from very light to quite heavy, although many good golfers prefer a heavier club to assist making a smooth, rhythmic motion.

Above left: The lie angle of a putter is also important. The head of the putter should sit flat on the ground. This putter has most of its weight at the heel and toe to prevent it twisting.

Above right: As with other clubs, try a variety of clubs on a green before making any decision.

Left: When you've sampled some putters, you will develop a favourite. Now it's down to good technique and reading the line of the putts – so read on.

PRO TIP

Just like any other club in your bag, a putter also has a lie angle, and having the correct one for you is vital to playing successfully on the greens. Choose a lie angle that sets your eyes over the ball when you adopt your posture. That's the secret to aiming correctly.

ADVANCED BALL CONTROL

◆◆◆◆◆

*To master the complexities
of this game you will need to be
able to curve the ball at will,
hit it high, low, stop it quickly,
and much more…*

THE DRAW SHOT

◆◆◆◆◆

A draw is a shot that propels the ball from right to left and it can increase distance, because the ball will generally run well when it lands. So it's a handy shot if you are looking to increase your length with the driver, fairway woods and long irons. The shape of the shot also helps you to avoid trouble off the tee, or play around hazards from the fairway.

I N ADDITION, a draw has a lower flight path, so it's an essential shot to have in your bag for windy days.

In order to hit the draw correctly, you must swing more in-to-out than normally, and develop some feel for how to shape the shot.

UNIQUE SWINGPATH

How do you produce the unique swingpath of a draw? Start with your alignment, pointing your feet, hips and shoulders slightly right of the target – or in what is often referred to as a 'closed' stance. But don't overdo it. Unless you are trying to bend the ball dramatically around an obstacle, the standard draw requires that you aim right by only about five degrees.

Next, set the ball back in your stance by about an inch to an inch and a half (3 to 4cm) from where you would normally place it for the club you are about to hit. This will encourage you to hit the ball from the inside.

Finally, adjust your grip by turning your hands to the right, or more underneath the club – this is often called a 'strong' grip. But be careful because overdoing this can easily turn a draw into a hook!

In fact, it's vital to experiment with various grip positions when you practise hitting a draw. If you hit the ball with a natural fade, or tend to slice it, drawing the ball will be difficult for you.

But mastering this shot can be fun. If you slice, trying to draw the ball is both challenging and rewarding, as you learn how

To play the draw shot, allow your hands to move slightly to the right on the grip.

The draw shot

to produce the opposite effect, which can also lead to hitting a straighter ball.

HOW TO HIT THE DRAW

In order to encourage an in-to-out swingpath, I tell golfers to imagine they are standing on a clockface with 12 o'clock being on the target-line straight ahead. Aiming the club at 1 o'clock, you want to take your swing back to 7 o'clock, then fire through to 1.

But why are you aiming at 1 o'clock rather than closing the face or squaring it to the target, which is the traditional way of teaching the draw?

I believe that if you see the clubface sitting closed to your swingpath, then you'll tend to swing to the left. But if you open the clubface a bit and aim at the 1 o'clock position, then you are already thinking in-to-out.

I also do not think that a golfer should do anything extraordinary on the backswing when learning a draw. I make a conventional backswing, then think about swinging the club from the inside on the throughswing, trying to let it drop in relatively close to my body. I promote this feeling by keeping the right elbow fairly close to the side of my torso as I start through, while visualizing how the club should swing out to the right.

IMPART SIDESPIN

I think it also helps to imagine you are playing this shot with a table tennis bat, attempting to impart sidespin – which in this case will be anti-clockwise. We are trying to get draw spin here, swinging the club from the inside to the outside, coming from fairly close to the body to away.

So a little extra right hand does not hurt as you come through the ball. Conjure up the idea of the right hand at the bottom of the swing arc and focus on the impression of using a table tennis bat. Looking at it another way, it's much like putting forehand topspin on a tennis ball.

Obviously, it is important that your hands are very free. A bit more release in the right hand than usual will not do any harm in developing the feel of a draw. But if you lock up in the hands, you'll lose confidence as you come through and block the ball miles to the right.

Remembering this is especially important if you tend to slice.

Below: Place the ball slightly (around an inch) further back in your stance.

Below: Aim slightly right of your target and hit from 7 o'clock to 1 o'clock. Swinging out to the right will help impart draw spin and move the ball from right to left.

KEYS TO LEARNING THE DRAW

◆ ◆ ◆ ◆ ◆

Try putting an umbrella into the ground just in front of your left foot to encourage the idea of swinging in-to-out. Now you must swing out from the right of the umbrella to avoid hitting it, and not allow the club to come back inside.

LAYING CLUBS on the ground is another way to groove an inside-to-out swingpath. Put one club near your feet, aiming slightly to the right of the target. Then put another club on the other side of the golf ball, pointing farther right of the target. Now swing along the lines of the club that is next to the ball to get the feel for the correct swingpath.

VISUALIZING THE SHOT

It's important to visualize any shot, but particularly so for the draw. You have to see this shot in order to feel it, imagining how it will bend from right to left. But unless that flight path is very clear in your mind, you should not even attempt to play a draw.

Think of it this way. Your brain can trigger a reflex in your body, which helps develop feel for the shot. And if you can feel the proper action for making the shot, then you can impart that to your arms and hands, which will work the club across the ball –

like that table tennis shot hitting the ball with sidespin.

But you also have to know where you want the ball to start. You must feel it starting out to the right, then working its way back around to the target. I cannot emphasize that enough. You must really feel that in order to execute this shot properly, producing a movement that allows you to swing down the right path.

REMAINING CONFIDENT

Golfers often lose confidence in their ability to hit a draw just when they get to the top of the backswing. If that happens, they pull right across the ball and hit it way left.

Again, it's because they do not want to swing the club out to the right, which goes against their natural instincts. You must have confidence to hit the ball out to the right and then let it come back again. And only with confidence will you allow yourself to swing with a free movement.

Step one – visualize the shot you intend to play.

Step two – once you've decided on the shot, commit yourself to a successful outcome. Here I'm trying to play the shot around a tree and bend the ball back to the left to hit the green.

Moving the ball right-to-left around an obstacle

Practising hitting shots with your right hand only is a great way to learn and understand the draw. Imagine you are playing a topspin table tennis shot as you make your swing and watch the ball move right to left.

PRACTISING THE DRAW

In order to learn this shot properly, you should practise first with only a 5- or 6-iron. You don't want to use a club with any more loft than that, because the more lofted a club is, the less potential you have to put spin on the ball.

That is why golfers generally hit their short irons straighter and more accurately. When the ball is going up, there's usually less sideways spin on it.

By contrast, the easiest clubs to draw (or fade) are the driver and long irons, because you can really get the ball spinning using less loft. However, you can also impart very violent spin with these clubs, so be careful.

HIT HALFSWINGS

Hit the 5- or 6-iron with little halfswings, concentrating on the swingpath to get a concept of how to impart spin – and gain an appreciation of how spin works. Again, this drill is about building a mental impression that you can transfer into the proper body movements.

Focus on your right hand, and how it has to work through the ball to create anti-clockwise spin.

Do this for some time and don't rush it, until, very gradually, you start to see the ball

moving from right to left. When that happens, you can start increasing the length of your swing, working slowly up to a full swing.

When playing a draw from the tee, position the ball on the far left of the tee box. You can then swing to the right which will encourage the draw shot.

PRO TIP

In order to promote the idea of hitting a draw when you are teeing off, tee the ball really high. That will automatically force you to sweep through the ball and encourage a feeling of hitting around it.

THE FADE SHOT

◆ ◆ ◆ ◆ ◆

Most players already naturally hit a fade, or its ugly sibling, the slice.
Lee Trevino, the master of hitting the ball left-to-right, once said that you
can talk to a fade but you can't talk to a hook. He's got a point.

LIKE A slice, a hook will make the ball run into all sorts of trouble. But when you hit the ball with a soft fade, at least you know the ball is going to stop nicely.

That's the beauty of this shot. The fade is ideal when you are faced with a left-to-right dogleg from the tee, when you have to bend the ball the same way around a hazard, or when you need to get more height to clear a tree and land the ball softly.

HIGH SHOT

Unlike the draw, the fade is a high shot that will not run very much when the ball reaches the ground. That makes it a great shot for long approaches to the green, but much trickier to use in the wind.

That's the good news. The bad news is that the average golfer will not get as much distance with a fade. And since most golfers lack some penetration with their shots anyway, always playing a fade is not desirable. In fact, most golfers would be better off trying to generate a draw in their swing, and using that particular option as their normal shot.

Having said that, knowing how to fade the ball is necessary for a variety of situations and absolutely essential if you truly want to improve your game.

HOW TO HIT A FADE

To hit a fade, I first open my stance by moving my front foot back of the target line. Aiming left, I align my feet, hips and shoulders in an open stance that points to 11 o'clock on the imaginary clockface.

In terms of swingpath, you want to think about moving out-to-in, pulling the club across the ball from 5 to 11 o'clock. That will impart clockwise spin.

If you tee the ball on the right-hand side of the teeing ground, it will encourage you to aim left and hit the fade shot.

How to play the fade

When you play the fade shot, aim slightly left of the target, move your grip fractionally to the left (a weaker grip), play the ball slightly further forward in your stance and picture the ball moving left-to-right.

ADJUSTED GRIP

The next thing you should do is to adjust your grip. If you naturally draw the ball, you will have to turn your hands round to the left – or 'weaken' your grip. This may be an advantage for some, but if you already hit the ball from left to right – or with a fade – it's important not to overdo this adjustment.

Opening your hands – or moving them more to the left – could produce a massive slice.

Remember that every change we make to create a golf shot has to be relative to *your*

game. So for the natural slicer, simply opening the stance a bit and aiming slightly left might be enough to produce the correct swingpath.

BALL POSITION

But let's assume you hit the ball straight and go from there. To hit a fade, especially if you want more height, means playing the ball a touch more forward in your stance than you would normally. Depending on where you start from, putting it about an inch (2.5cm) further forward should be enough. In simple terms, that means playing it off your left heel.

However, if you already play the ball from inside your left heel, you do not need to move it further forward for a fade. Playing any shot with the ball too far up in your stance will cause you to pull it – or hit straight left.

Left: To encourage the fade you can play the ball slightly further forwards – but don't overdo it!

Above: Weaken the grip by turning the hands fractionally to the left.

KEYS TO THE FADE SWING

◆ ◆ ◆ ◆ ◆

I like to play a fade a little bit more from my left side.
After taking an open set-up, I swing back along the line of my stance,
without modifying anything in my backswing. Since I am aiming left,
I have already swung naturally outside the target line.

BUT WHEN I come through the ball, I want to cut across the same line and move the club inside by delaying the release of the clubhead just a fraction.

RELAXED HAND

How do I accomplish that? I first relax my right hand at address, and then grip the club a little bit tighter with the last three fingers of my left hand – the little, ring and middle fingers. In other words, the right hand stays very light, while the leading hand grips just a bit firmer.

When I come through the ball, I then try to feel as though I'm delaying the release of the clubhead just a bit, or simply preventing the club from coming through as early as normal. That should be enough to hit slightly across the ball.

However, this does not mean that I do not release the clubhead! What it means is the release comes just slightly later than it would for a regular shot. Apart from that, I just swing normally.

AVOIDING TROUBLE

Professional golfers routinely move the ball in varying directions to avoid trouble on one side of a golf course or the other. If the trouble is on the right, they'll hit a draw. If it's on the left-hand side, they'll play a fade. The key is actually to start the ball towards the trouble spot, then move it away.

The 18th hole on the championship West Course at Wentworth is a good example. This is a classic set-up for a fade because the hole doglegs left to right, with a big bunker on the left. Most pros will hit the ball at the bunker and then let it slide.

To encourage the fade, grip the club slightly firmer with the top three fingers of the left hand. Keep the right hand relaxed.

When you are trying to fade the ball off the tee with a wood, tee the ball down (above). This is especially useful when you're under pressure and there's trouble on the left. By teeing the ball down you are almost certain to fade the ball with a driver.

To play the fade shot, imagine you are swinging from 5 to 11 o'clock, moving the club across the ball on an out-to-in path. Feel more left-side control as you swing forwards with the left hand leading the clubhead through the ball.

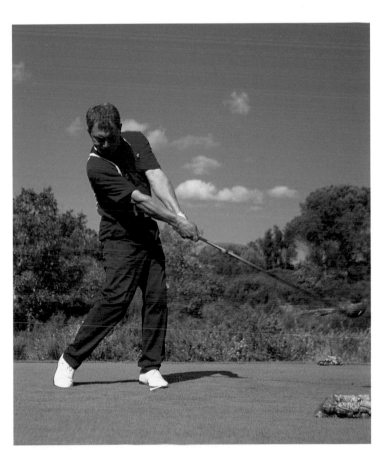

So if you ever play Wentworth, I would suggest you tee the ball low on the 18th, get out your driver, and hit it straight at the bunker, gripping a little bit tighter with those last three fingers of the left hand

You will pull the club through the ball as you do normally. But because you're hitting with the leading hand gripping just slightly tighter than the other hand, the clubface will come through a split second later. That will impart the necessary spin to curve the ball away from the bunker and into the middle of the fairway.

USE LESS LOFT

If you're hitting a wood and want almost to ensure you fade the ball, the less loft the better. In other words, if you normally hit a 3-wood off the tee, take a driver. And if you usually employ a 5-wood off the fairway, you might want to drop down to a 3.

The 3-wood is easier to fade because it makes the ball spin more than the loft on a 5-wood. In addition, you might even try hitting a driver off the fairway. To hit a draw in that situation is virtually impossible, but you have a chance if you try to fade the ball.

PRO TIP

If you are on the tee and want to make sure you do not hook the ball because there is real trouble down the left-hand side, tee the ball low and take out your driver. Now think about hitting a fade. With the ball so low to the ground, and the driver in your hand, it's almost impossible to hook. Instead, your natural instinct will produce a fade, because you'll be thinking you virtually have to swing from out-to-in on the ball to make it get airborne.

TAILWIND ADVANTAGES

◆ ◆ ◆ ◆ ◆

Great golfers learn how to use the wind to their advantage, and minimize the damage when that is not possible. So do not let the wind play on your mind, or you'll lose confidence – which leads to tension and ultimately a breakdown in your swing. Playing in the wind can be both challenging and fun, if you know what you are doing.

A TAILWIND CAN help you to increase your distance dramatically and actually assist you to hit your shots in a straighter line. On the other hand, hitting into the wind can reduce your distance, but aid you in stopping the ball quickly on the green and even impart some backspin.

Crosswinds are trickier. But once you learn how to hit into the windstream correctly and then let it carry your ball, you will be on the way to lowering your scores – even when the wind blows a gale.

USING A TAILWIND

Most golfers automatically feel more comfortable with the wind at their backs because they know it will help them hit the ball further. However, unless they understand and employ certain advanced techniques for hitting in the wind, they'll never fully capitalize on that obvious advantage.

Let's say you are on the tee of a long par four where you would normally play a driver. Now, of course, every golfer knows that hitting a 3-wood off the tee generally guarantees more accuracy and control when it is struck properly, though distance is sacrificed.

But in this situation hitting a 3-wood rather than the driver is the best play, because the added loft will get the ball up higher and into the prevailing wind. In addition, even if you do not get a perfect strike on the ball, less sidespin will be imparted, and the ball will go straighter and further.

Decisions, decisions – choosing the right club is crucial in windy conditions.

Far left: A tailwind will help to increase your distance and straighten your shots

Left: Looking at the tops of the trees will tell you more about the wind than conditions at ground level do. Use the knowledge to your advantage.

Far left: Wearing a hat can stop you hair blowing around – not that I have to worry too much about that!

Left: A stable base to your golf swing is very important. If it's windy, I increase the width of my stance.

PRO TIP

Not enough players practise in the wind. If you are on the course on a windy day and it's quiet, drop some balls and experiment with a few clubs to see what effect the wind has on how each performs, and how the wind affects your natural ball flight.

The same principle applies once you are on the fairway. Where you would normally use a 3-wood, you can now try the 5- or even 7-wood and get just as much distance – if not more because they are easier to hit – with the added benefit of more control.

STRAIGHTER FLIGHT

A tailwind will also straighten out your natural ball flight – whether you hit with a bit of fade or draw – because the wind lessens the amount of spin. That makes for a more penetrating hit and allows you to place the ball more accurately for your next shot.

Make sure you aim for the side of the fairway that will allow you to run the ball up to the green – using perhaps a long bump and run shot. Remember that you will never stop the ball on the putting surface with a high wedge shot in a tailwind.

You should also know that the ball will kick and run on from your tee shot, so mentally you have to allow for that. As for approach shots, a strong tailwind will produce enough boost to move a 7- or even 8-iron shot 150 to 200 yards (137 to 183m).

Golfers often cannot convince themselves of that fact. They may take the correct club, but when they get to the top of their backswing, they suddenly panic and think they have not got enough club, thus forcing the shot.

Assess the effect of the wind, select a club and then keep faith with the shot you have decided to hit.

Keep the swing compact and this will help you to maintain control while others around you are flailing away.

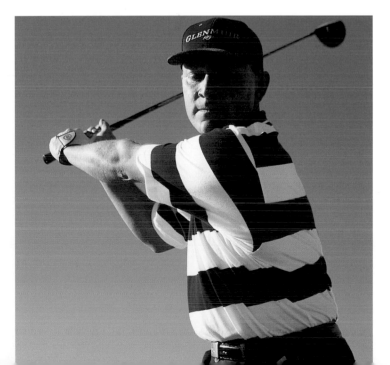

HIT SOFT INTO A HEADWIND

◆ ◆ ◆ ◆ ◆

Hitting into a headwind will increase the spin on the ball, which is an excellent incentive for firing confidently at the pin, and trusting the ball to stop quickly on the green. But if you are on the tee or facing a long shot from the fairway, you have to remember that this aspect of hitting into the wind will exaggerate any problems you have with the long woods and irons.

I F YOU hit a driver with a bit of draw, playing with the wind in your face could change that shot into a hook. Alternatively, if you hit the ball with a nice little fade, that could become an ugly slice. You have to make allowances for these tendencies, or you will pay a significant price.

PLAY IT SAFE AND SMOOTH

Take the safest route up the fairway that you can, choosing one side or the other while accepting the fact that you will lose considerable distance – perhaps as much as 50 to 75 yards (45 to 69m) on a drive. But less length is better than parking the ball in the rough or something worse.

Try teeing the ball higher than normal, then think about picking it clean off the top in an attempt to hit a penetrating shot that flies low into the wind.

Tempo is also a key here. You have to maintain your composure, and keep a smooth, even rhythm to your swing. Losing it in the wind can destroy your game very, very quickly.

THREE-CLUB WIND

Once you are down on the fairway, play very conservatively and remember that you might have to hit one, two or three more clubs than you usually would to achieve certain distances. How often have you heard people say that a 30mph (50km/h) wind is 'a three-club wind?' If you've ever played in such winds, you know the truth of that phrase all too well.

Tee the ball high and aim to sweep the ball clean off the tee.

A combination of stability and compactness are the keys to playing in the wind.

Good balance in windy conditions

wind direction

Hitting a golf ball into a headwind is one situation where playing the long irons, rather than utility woods, is a good idea. Using a 5- or 7-wood in strong winds is not advisable because the ball will just shoot into the air.

But the 3- and 4-irons can really play their parts superbly in these situations, because they will help you keep the ball flat.

Even a driver off the fairway is worth trying, if you have practised the shot on the range. In an emergency, with the wind against you, hit a little three-quarter swing with the big club, trying to keep your movement as smooth as possible.

Don't worry about mis-hitting the ball, because you might get a better result than using something like a 5-wood, since the ball will stay flat. But even if you top it, that's better than hitting the ball up in the air, where it can go just about any place.

STAYING SAFE

Whatever club you use on the fairway, be certain to look for the safest route to approach the green – and don't try anything too ambitious. If the hole is a par four, expect that it might well take you three shots, or perhaps even four, just to reach the green.

Consider this: if you two-putt from there, it's a six, rather than the eight or nine you're more likely to record if you fly out of bounds or into significant trouble.

Remember, you are going to have a hole somewhere else on the golf course where the wind is with you, and you will have a chance to repair the damage to your score.

It's tough – but always visualize a positive outcome to your shot, even when the wind is howling around your ears and burning your face.

DRIVER OFF THE DECK

I would never recommend hitting a driver off the fairway in normal circumstances – especially for the beginner or high handicap player who should also avoid using a 3-wood anywhere except from the tee. But if you are an experienced golfer, possess a solid, repeatable swing, and have the confidence to attempt this shot, I recommend it for playing in the wind. The first thing to consider is the lie. Hitting a driver off the fairway demands an excellent lie, so always avoid a tight lie or any situation where the ball is sitting even slightly down. Put the ball about an inch (2.5cm) farther back in your stance than you would off the tee and try to keep your hands slightly ahead of the ball at impact. If you make solid contact, the ball should take off with a low, penetrating line of flight.

SWING KEYS TO APPLYING BACKSPIN

◆ ◆ ◆ ◆ ◆

The key to applying backspin is how you develop a very precise strike on the ball. You have to make sure you hit the ball before you hit anything else. If you hit the ground just slightly before you hit the ball, you will fail to create backspin.

ONE WAY I encourage a precise strike is by looking more closely at the top of the ball, much as I do for a fairway bunker shot. Focusing in this way will help to ensure that you make clean contact.

I also play a more out-to-in type of swing, almost trying intentionally to fade the ball. That makes me think about hitting down and across the ball. Coming at the ball from out-to-in gives me a better chance of hitting the ball crisply and sharply.

TAKE A DIVOT

I also try to take a divot. With the shorter irons, I'm already hitting on a slightly downward path, and this helps me create backspin as it will make the ball spin up the clubface. But I would add a note of caution here. Hitting down on the ball too much runs the risk of chopping the clubface into the ground – either before or after impact with the ball.

Both mistakes will affect the strike considerably, and you will not get a positive result. Remember that you want to take a divot, but you do not want simply to hit down, so ensure that you hit down and *forward* towards your target. As with any golf shot, you always want to be going forwards and through the ball.

In addition, because you are using a short, lofted club, you will be bent over more. So be careful not to exaggerate your action too much. The divot does not need to be half the size of the state of Ohio – or even Surrey!

To apply increased backspin, you need to open your stance, with your weight slightly favouring your left side. Take the club away with your arms and break your wrists early to produce a sharp downward strike into the ball. You should use a three-quarter swing, keep your hands ahead of the clubface, and keep your weight transfer down to a minimum.

To help create backspin I open my stance, keep my weight forward and break my wrists quite early in my backswing. This results in a sharp downward strike on the ball.

The priority here is not distance but a clean strike. A more compact swing helps you to make a precise strike, because, with your weight favouring the left side and your hands ahead of the club, you will naturally hit the ball with a descending blow.

Alternatively, if you try to lift the ball with your club, your weight will probably stay on the back foot, which will cause you to hit the ground first with the clubhead or top the ball.

Trying to scoop the ball upwards is the major fault of most golfers in this situation. They forget the great paradox of golf – that you must strike down to hit the ball up, letting the loft of the clubface produce a high-flying shot.

KEEP IT CLEAN

A clean ball and clubface is also essential to applying backspin. Make sure you check your ball whenever you can during a round, and see that the grooves in your clubface are free of dirt and grass. I am in the habit of tidying up my wedges after every strike with a groove cleaner or a tee peg, while also making sure the clubface in general is clean.

Always remember to carry a towel on your bag for this purpose as well. Even in dry conditions, it is important to clean the ball and your clubs regularly.

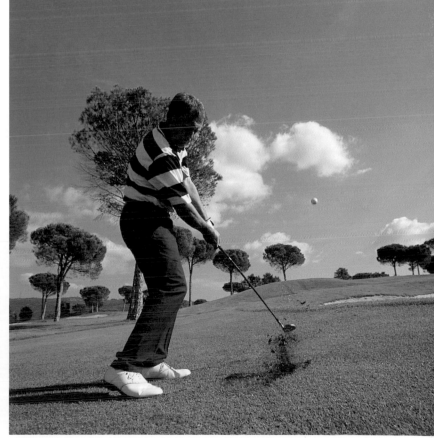

THE BUMP AND RUN

◆ ◆ ◆ ◆ ◆

The bump and run is an effective shot when you are trying to keep the ball low under the wind, playing off hard ground, or simply trying to run the ball up to a green. The shot is much easier to judge and control than a high pitch, and is ideal when you do not have to fly bunkers, water or rough to reach the green.

MOST GOLFERS associate this shot with links courses, where it is often employed to avoid tricky winds. Playing target golf on such courses can be a disaster. When the ball gets airborne, it can be blown off line, especially with a wedge.

But the bump and run can be used on any course under the right conditions – or the wrong ones for that matter.

THIN HOPES

In the summer, when the fairways tend to dry out, the bump and run is also useful because it allows for a wide margin of error. Even if you thin the ball, it will still run forwards along your intended line, perhaps accomplishing pretty much what you had hoped for anyway.

Using the bump and run to an uphill green is also a great idea, since it's easy to misjudge the distance and park a lofted shot

on the bank and short – or fly the green completely.

You can use a variety of clubs for the bump and run, and hit the shot anywhere from 60 to 160 yards (55 to 145m).

THE APPROACH SHOT

As with any golf shot, club selection is the first important decision you must make. You can play a bump and run with anything from a sand wedge to a 6-iron, depending on what you want to do.

These are two clubs you may consider when playing the bump and run shot.

Here I'm playing a shot from around 65 yards (60m) from the hole.

Bump and run

Try practising a variety of bump and run shots at the range to learn the best choices for you in different situations.

Selecting the right club will have a lot to do with how far you want the ball to fly before it starts running, or what you want it to clear initially. If you are playing a links course and have a lot of humps and bumps ahead, you may want to take many of them out by flying the ball further. That may demand a wedge.

But if you really want to keep the ball flat to the ground, or low and running most of the way, then you might choose a 6-iron.

CONTROL AND FEEL

I'll use a 60-yard (55m) shot to the green as a typical example.

In that case, you might want the ball to fly 40 yards (37m) and roll 20 yards (18m). Take out the wedge and choke halfway down the grip for better control and feel. Then open your stance, with the hips and feet pointing slightly left of the target, but the shoulders remaining parallel to the target line.

The shoulders should be positioned as they would be for a conventional shot because the last thing I want to do is to hit the ball with an out-to-in swingpath.

Ideally, I want the club actually to come from a slightly in-to-out direction, which will help get the ball running.

GOING LOW

Now I set the ball back in my stance, from the centre to slightly behind that, which helps make the ball fly lower. In turn, my hands are set ahead of the clubhead, which helps deloft the club and also helps make the ball run low.

Finally, I set my weight towards the left side and keep it there. I don't want much weight transfer when making this shot.

BUMP AND RUN WITH A PUTTER

A shot that often can be very successful is a bump and run with a putter. I have used my putter from up to 50 yards (45m) from the green if there are no hazards, conditions are dry and the grass is short.

The length of the back- and throughswings should control the distance you will hit the ball.

Playing the ball along the ground with a putter from up to 50 yards (45m) can be very successful. Ensure that the ground is dry and that there are no obstacles (such as sprinkler heads) in between you and the hole. And remember, never up – never in!

SWING KEYS TO THE BUMP AND RUN

◆◆◆◆◆

Once I am set up properly for the bump and run, I plan to take a half- to three-quarter swing – depending on the length of my approach – trying to keep even and balanced throughout.

THE BEST way to do that is to think about matching the length of the throughswing to the backswing. I also want to take the body out of this movement and just swing with the arms and hands.

SMOOTHLY DONE

A smooth, unhurried tempo is essential. It's very easy to rush these shots, especially with a little wind around. The tendency is to get forwards too quickly.

At the same time, you want to ensure you accelerate through the ball, with the feeling that you are almost squeezing it between the clubface and turf.

Remember, you want to create overspin on the ball to get it running, and from your set-up, you will naturally be bringing the clubface from in-to-out – helping you nip the ball off the ground.

POINTS SKYWARD

Think of this shot as dominated by the left side. What you do not want to do is to lift the ball by using too much right hand. So keep both hands ahead of the clubface, but lead the shot with the back of your left hand.

You don't want to break your wrists too much on the backswing, and you don't want to release the right arm on the throughswing. So visualize that, at the end of your swing, the back of your left hand will be facing up at the sky.

Letting the wrists break would lead to a chopping action on the ball, rather than promoting the idea of squeezing it off the turf to get a nice, flat trajectory.

THE LONGER APPROACH

You can use the bump and run from 100 yards (91m) out to even 160 (145m), employing a sand wedge down to a 6-iron although with the former you will need to substantially deloft the face. The approach on this shot is similar to when using a wedge from only 60 yards (55m).

Again, you want to take an open stance, but with the shoulders still parallel to the target line. Then use a three-quarter swing, with your weight and hands forward. Try to squeeze the ball off the turf by hitting down with a firm left wrist, making sure the swingpath is slightly in-to-out. Finish with your left wrist pointing at the sky.

VISUALIZING THE SHOT

Once again visualization plays its part. This is especially important on a links-type course

Below left: When playing the bump and run, keep your hands well ahead of the clubhead as you make your throughswing.

Below: Remember to allow for contours in the ground as they will affect the run of your ball.

The bump and run requires you to make a low takeaway. Keep the weight principally on your left foot and then pull the club forwards with the hands staying well ahead of the clubhead through impact, as shown here.

with a lot of humps and bumps. If you were to hit a lofted club in this situation, and the ball came down on the wrong hump, it could fly off sideways or even worse. Running it in is a better option, because the ball can roll along with the contours of the land.

So pick a spot where you want the ball initially to come down, and try to imagine how it will react. Then focus on that spot — much as you would for a chip — and hit your shot.

HELP FOR THE WEEKEND GOLFER

The bump and run is a great shot if you only play golf once a week. Trying to play target golf without hours of practice is difficult. But if you hit more low runners than high-flying pitches during a round, you have the advantage of probably succeeding even if you mis-hit the ball.

With the bump and run, a semi-thinned shot will still produce a half-decent result — you are already anticipating running the ball.

When the ground is hard and dry, it's much safer and more predictable to keep the ball low. With the grass reasonably fine, the ball will trundle along nicely, reacting almost as it would on the green.

THE LOB SHOT

◆ ◆ ◆ ◆ ◆

The lob is one of the toughest shots in golf. But with the proper technique and lots of practice, many golfers can learn how to execute it consistently. You need this shot when you have to play over a hazard and then stop the ball quickly in a small landing area around the pin – sometimes as close as just a few feet away.

SO THE lob is a shot that you are sometimes *forced* to play, rather than one you might occasionally choose. I play this shot from only five to 15 yards (4.5 to 13.5m) away – maybe 20 yards (18m) at the most. Trying to hit a lob shot from much farther than that is getting into very dangerous territory.

SPECIALIST CLUB

The advent of the lob wedge has helped every golfer play this shot better. Of course, the pros can still open up their sand wedges and play the lob shot with great precision. But the average golfer risks thinning the ball if he tries a similar technique.

A sand wedge has a high degree of bounce, so opening the blade and trying to play this shot from low-cut grass, a tight lie or hardpan can be extremely problematic. However, if the lie is good and there is a lot of grass under the ball, then a sand wedge might work for you.

HITTING THE LOB

Open your stance, with your feet, hips and shoulders pointing left by 15 to 20 degrees. You must aim that far left to compensate for how far you are going to open the face of the sand wedge. Now open up your wedge by as much as 8 degrees, depending on how high you want to lift the ball – really laying the clubface open.

Play the ball off the inside of your left heel or front foot, angling the club for an out-to-in swingpath with your weight favouring the left foot in a ratio of about 60/40.

Below: This shot requires the left hand to be in control through the ball.

Below left: Almost all professionals carry a lob wedge these days.

Left: Only try the lob shot if you have grass beneath the ball. Don't even consider it if you're sitting on hard ground.

The left side in control

When I play the lob shot, I try to imagine my left arm pulling the club through the ball, with the back of the left hand slicing across the ball. The back of the left hand should be pointing towards the sky at the end of the swing.

Below: With the lob wedge I generally don't need to open the face as the club is very lofted anyway.

REALLY STABLE

You want real stability with this shot. Try to keep as centred as possible and keep your head still and your weight towards your left foot.

Take a three-quarter backswing with a sharp pickup of the wrists. Then really try to feel the butt of the club coming through ahead of the clubhead, so that you pull across the ball.

I try to imagine almost slicing under the ball with the back of my left hand. That will help me shoot the ball quickly up in the air with lots of backspin, then let it drop down very softly.

MORE HEIGHT

I can get even more height with a lob wedge because the club has so much more loft. I also don't need to open the face quite so much – if at all. The rest of the technique employed to hit the lob shot stays pretty much the same. But, like any shot, make sure you practise it regularly to build confidence.

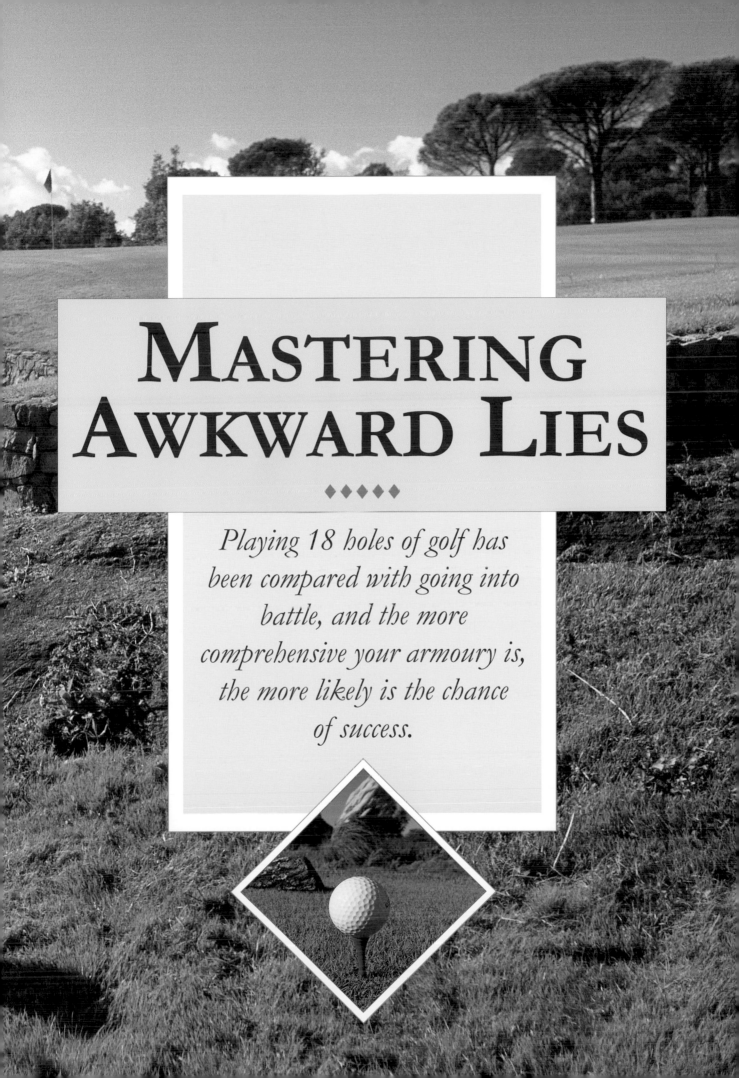

MASTERING
AWKWARD LIES

◆ ◆ ◆ ◆ ◆

Playing 18 holes of golf has been compared with going into battle, and the more comprehensive your armoury is, the more likely is the chance of success.

HOW TO ESCAPE FROM HEAVY ROUGH

◆ ◆ ◆ ◆ ◆

The sand wedge is particularly useful from thick rough because it has a heavy soleplate which helps you swing through grass, weeds, brambles and whatever other nasty stuff is around your ball. A golf club can be stopped cold in the rough, and if that happens, the ball will not move an inch! Or it might just pop out a few feet in front of you.

S O YOU need a heavy club that can lift the ball out. In addition, you have to swing through the grass behind the ball before making contact, which can snag the club and close down the clubface as you make your strike. When that happens, the club is effectively de-lofted, and the ball might not get airborne at all.

In fact, the ball may even be driven further into the grass. I have seen fellow pros hit a ball in the rough that moves only three or four inches (8 to 10cm), sometimes even going downwards into further trouble.

If the grass is deep enough, the ball can even become lost!

OPEN THE CLUBFACE

In heavy rough, even a sand wedge will tend to snag, closing down the face of the club. So open the blade up just a bit to compensate for this, then play the shot the same way you would in a bunker. And remember to open the face first, then take your grip, so that the club is set correctly in your hands, open by 5 to 10 degrees. Finally, take a nice full swing and try to hit right through the ball.

Even if the club eventually does get snagged and stops, focus on trying to go through the ball – that will usually get the ball out.

Play to a point on the fairway that is not too ambitious. Unless you have to, do not try to hit the ball over more rough, because you often will not be successful.

If you find yourself in thick rough, the sand wedge is a good option to get the ball back into play.

Below: No matter how thick the rough is, try to follow through.

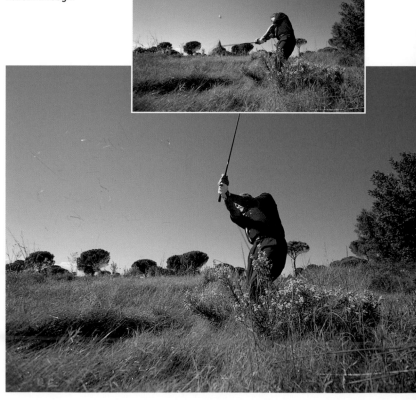

PLAYING OUT OF LIGHT ROUGH

◆ ◆ ◆ ◆ ◆

Landing in the rough is not always a disaster. If you can see even a little bit of the back of the ball, you have some hope of hitting a positive shot. But you still need a club with a great deal of loft. An 8-iron is as low as you should go when hitting out of difficult rough. However, if you hit an 8 iron from the rough, bear in mind that you'll probably get a flyer.

A FLYER IS when the grass comes between the ball and the clubface, which prevents you getting any backspin on the ball. The ball might literally shoot off the club, going 30 or 40 per cent farther than it would normally.

Sometimes, that can work to your advantage. If you normally hit an 8-iron 130-150 yards (119 to 137m), a flyer may well send it 170-190 yards (155 to 174m) – especially if the fairway is running a bit. If you have a long approach to the green, that might be a big help in saving a stroke. But a flyer can also work against you, so take the added length that may result into consideration when hitting from the rough. Knowing the ball will run significantly when it lands at least helps you to plan how to execute the shot.

If you're playing a short approach to the green, remember that you will not be able to stop the ball unless the surface is very soft. Instead, you may have to run the ball up to the green.

Below: Remember when playing from the rough, the ball will run much further than when you are playing from the fairway.

Left and above: If your ball is sitting in the first cut of the rough, a long iron cannot be used. Therefore, depending on the length of the shot and the lie of the ball, consider a lofted iron. For longer shots use a 5- or 7-wood.

USING UTILITY WOODS FROM THE ROUGH

◆ ◆ ◆ ◆ ◆

A 7-wood is an innovation that can help tremendously when playing out of the rough. You may also want to try one of the newer 9-woods or even an 11-wood. These days, a lot of women and senior players use such clubs but many low handicap and pro golfers are also increasingly finding them useful.

I N FACT, a 7-wood is probably a better club for the average golfer to carry in his bag than a difficult 3-iron. Utility woods are much easier to use in all sorts of situations around the course, but especially from the rough. However, employing a wood depends on the type of lie in which you find your ball. In order to use a fairway wood from the rough, you must see some of the back of the ball. If you cannot see any ball, then forget about using the wood.

SNAG PROOF

The reason utility woods can work out of the rough is because the clubhead is rounded, and sometimes has a 'V-shaped' sole that will not get snagged in the grass. Also, the clubface is lofted and will elevate the ball very quickly. The quicker the ball gets up, the less it tends to fly sideways.

When using the utility woods in the rough, you should exert slightly more grip pressure than usual. You want to get down

Above: When playing from the rough, you will need to hold the club firmly to avoid the club getting snagged by the grass.

Above: Utility woods are ideal for long shots from semi-rough.

Right: Trying to lead the club with the left hand (like playing a pitch shot) creates more of an out-to-in swing – this helps get a sharper strike in longer grass.

into the ball and through it, leading with your left hand.

SWINGPATH IN THE ROUGH

Whether you use a wood or an iron from the rough, you want to swing more out-to-in, rather than the normal swingpath of in-to-in. You are trying to come at the ball from the outside, so you should take the club back slightly outside the line and pick it up a little more abruptly than with your normal swing – somewhat like a bunker shot.

Then think about trying to angle the club down, imagining you are almost hitting a slice, moving the ball from left to right as much as possible. The more you slice across the target line, the more chance you have of getting a sharp strike on the back of the ball, which will get it up quickly and send it flying forwards, imparting the proper flight to the ball.

Because of this swingpath, you might even get a flyer with a wood. In that case, the ball could travel as far as it would from a normal lie on the fairway. But again, it takes practice to judge these shots properly.

PRO TIP

It's essential to practise hitting balls from the rough. If you don't, once you get into the stuff on a course, you will not know what to do. You'll have no feel for the situation, and you will not be able to assess the shot and choose the right method for escaping from trouble.

Find an empty field in which to practise, or any area where the grass has not been mown. Try a variety of shots and use your sand wedge or utility wood. Another option is to use the rough on your local golf course when playing on a quiet day, or the unkept areas around the practice grounds. Since they are often not maintained, the club probably will not mind you doing this. But it pays to ask first.

When I'm playing from the rough, I take the club back a little outside the line – aim a little left and visualize a fade shot.

At the top of the backswing, maintain your composure – all too often players panic when playing from the rough and rush into the shot.

As you swing through the ball, try to come slightly out-to-in, cutting down and across the ball.

As you swing through the ball, lead with the left hand, as though you're playing a pitch or bunker shot. This will produce a 'cutting' action ensuring a sharper strike on the ball.

Swing through the ball to a positive and athletic finish and watch your ball sail towards the green.

USING A LOB WEDGE FROM A GREENSIDE BUNKER

◆ ◆ ◆ ◆ ◆

When you have to get the ball up quickly from a fairway bunker, you might consider using a lob wedge, which many players now carry in their bags. The lob wedge can have 60 to 64 degrees of loft, whereas a sand wedge only has 56 degrees of loft.

BUT FOR most golfers, the best aspect is that you do not have to open the face of a lob wedge, which is the whole reason to own one. A lob wedge can be used with the clubface sitting squarely, which makes it much easier to play through the ball. That can take a lot of pressure off a golfer who already has enough to worry about in a fairway bunker.

MORE LIFT

Of course, you can also open up a lob wedge for even more lift on the ball, but generally I would not recommend doing that. If you try to open up your lob wedge, you run the risk of hitting clean under the ball – with little or no forward momentum and leaving the ball in the bunker.

So take a conventional bunker set-up with the lob wedge, then play the shot with a square clubface, aiming the blade along the line of flight – while making sure you pull the club through the sand, moving forwards rather than down.

LOB WEDGE VERSUS SAND WEDGE

Why use a sand wedge at all if you now own a lob wedge?

A lob wedge generally does not have much of a flange on it – the thicker sole under a sand iron that is angled slightly to give the club bounce and that keeps it from burying itself in the sand.

A lob wedge can have a sharper soleplate, but it certainly will not have the reverse angle of a sand wedge. The sand iron is designed so that the back of the sole sits on the ground, while the front edge of the clubface is actually in the air – by as much as 20 degrees.

BOUNCING EDGE

That is what gives the sand wedge bounce. It is made that way so the back edge will hit the sand and not dig in. In effect, the bounce stops the club from burying itself in the sand, which causes the club to decelerate or even to stop.

So, if you use a lob wedge, keep the differences between the two clubs in mind. With a sand wedge, you can really splash into the bunker knowing that the bounce on the bottom of the club will help it keep moving. But with a lob wedge, the club may stop.

In fact, the lob wedge may just go downwards into the sand and sink in. As a result, make sure you drive through the sand more, moving forwards rather than down. Of course, you should still take some sand. Trying to hit too cleanly opens you up to the risk of thinning or semi-topping the ball.

Trust your lob wedge and swing forwards toward your intended target.

A lob wedge can have up to 64 degrees of loft – it is, therefore, ideal when you have to get the ball up quickly and land it softly.

A sand wedge can be used to play a very high shot but will need to be opened, making the shot more difficult.

Take the club back
outside the ball-to-
target line.

Make a full backswing.

As you swing through,
bring the club across the
ball swinging left.

Keep the hands ahead of
the clubhead as the club
swings through the ball.

Swing all the way
through to a complete
finish.

PLAY GREAT SHOTS FROM FAIRWAY BUNKERS

◆◆◆◆◆

*The standard fairway bunker generally has a much lower lip
than a pot bunker, rising to perhaps only four feet (1.2m) at most.
However, that is intimidating enough if you are the least bit unsure about
how to execute this shot. The problem is that you have to get the ball out
cleanly, and you probably still have a considerable distance to go
before landing it on the green.*

S O TAKE a deep breath and try to assess what you can and cannot do given your situation, while conjuring up a picture of a successful shot flying out of the bunker.

SIZING UP THE LIP

The first factor to take into consideration is how close you are to the front part of the bunker, or the lip. If you are only a few feet away, that will have a big influence on the shot, compared to a position at the back, which can almost take the face of the bunker out of play.

In the first instance, you may have to settle for a lofted club to clear the lip, while in the latter situation, you might even be able to use a 3-wood to achieve maximum distance.

ASSESSING THE LIE

The second factor to consider in fairway bunkers is the lie. This is a shot where you need to make clean contact with the ball. But if the ball is plugged in the sand in any way, that will be impossible. So take a sand wedge, play the ball out safe, and don't expect too much.

On the other hand, if you have a decent lie and some clearance, once again you might consider using a wood and going for the green.

Assessing the lie

Assess the lie before choosing your golf club. If the ball is sitting down in the sand, you will need to use a lofted club to get the ball out.

Choosing the angle

A trick to help get the ball up quickly, while still getting distance, is to take a lower number iron or wood and open the face. Aim left to compensate, otherwise the ball will end up in the rough on the right.

Fairway bunker shot

When I play a fairway bunker shot, I do the following: take aim, (open my clubface if necessary), embed my feet, make a three-quarter swing and look at the top of the ball – and then off you go. Good luck!

CLEARING THE FACE

When the lip of a fairway bunker is a factor, you want to choose a golf club that has sufficient loft on it, both to get the ball out and to cover the appropriate distance – without changing your golf swing. Tinkering with your swing puts you in unfamiliar territory, which is a double-whammy when you are already stranded in a fairway bunker. Performing a normal swing is difficult enough.

SOLVING A DILEMMA

How do you solve this dilemma? Let's say you have a shot that demands the distance of a 7-iron, but the height of a 9. To get the extra distance and height, try aiming left of the target, then open the clubface slightly and play the shot with a slight fade or even a small slice. This will produce a more lofted shot – but using your normal swing.

You should also try to focus on the top of the ball to avoid hitting it fat. And you should make sure that you have a decent footing in the sand so you do not slip. Using a three-quarter to full swing, try to ensure you get clean contact. Hitting the sand first will kill the shot.

But remember – don't be over-ambitious. If you choose a club with which it is almost impossible to get the appropriate lift, the ball will hit the face of the bunker and come back at you. Then you really are in serious trouble.

PLAYING FROM A DIVOT

◆ ◆ ◆ ◆ ◆

*The first problem when playing from a divot is usually a psychological one.
After walking down the fairway, you discover the ball is in a divot hole.
Even worse, unless the ball is sitting up on the front or back edge of the
divot, it will probably be below the level of the fairway.*

NOW you're frustrated – especially if you hit a good shot to get there in the first place. But if you start feeling sorry for yourself, you are likely to aggravate the problem even more. Landing in a divot happens, and it happens to everybody, which is something you have to accept and deal with appropriately. In fact, some would contend that hitting into a divot in the final round of 1998 US Open cost Payne Stewart that title. But a year later, Stewart came back and won the 1999 US Open.

So approach this shot positively. Playing from a divot is not impossible by any means. Here's how it's done.

THE APPROACH SHOT

In playing out of a divot, you are essentially trying to get your clubhead down into the divot hole, making as clean a contact with the ball as possible. Therefore, club selection is all-important – although distance is not the only factor.

On a par five or short par four, you are most likely to land in a divot within 100 yards (91m) of the green, which is where almost everyone's approach shot or drive finishes. But if the ball is sitting down in the divot hole – and a sand wedge is the right club for the distance to the green – you have a real problem.

The sand wedge is designed to bounce, rather than go down into a hole. So steer away from the sand wedge, or you will end up thinning the ball.

PLAYING WITH A LOB WEDGE

The lob wedge is a good choice for an approach shot from a divot. Position the ball back in your stance and close the face up a bit. In effect, that will make your lob wedge into a sand wedge, giving you the loft you are looking for without the bounce. And that will help you get the club down into the divot hole.

Keeping your hands fairly forward, favour your front foot with most of your weight, then try to concentrate on driving through the shot.

Use a three-quarter swing for a more

Playing from a divot isn't the easiest shot in golf, but if you use a lofted club, it need not become a disaster.

compact movement, which will help you to drive through the ball and downwards into the shot. I emphasize downwards because if the club brushes or sweeps across the surface of the fairway, you will merely top or thin the shot.

TAKE ANOTHER DIVOT

The key to this shot is to drive down into the ball and take another divot. In other words, if you are playing from a divot, you have to take another divot! However, I must warn you that the ball can shoot out of these lies and take off – or it can fly normally. It's difficult to judge.

MARGIN OF ERROR

So if you have an option in terms of where to land the ball on the green, I would definitely take aim at the broadest open area. You must not take the tightest line, such as over a bunker to a small landing area. You want plenty of space to give yourself a margin of error. Hitting a perfect shot from a divot is extremely ambitious so allow for some degree of error.

Besides the lob wedge, and depending on the situation, you might also consider playing an 8, 9 or pitching wedge. None of these clubs has any bounce on the sole. But stay away from the sand wedge!

Turning a disappointment into a success

GET OUT OF A RUT

Remember that to get out of a divot, you have to take another divot (see below). Many beginners and even some intermediate players often do not take divots after the ball because they lack confidence and have never learned how to hit an iron with a sharp, descending blow. To build that confidence – so you can strike firmly and take another divot when faced with this tricky shot – practise by putting a tee peg an inch or two in front of a ball on the practice range. Then focus on hitting down and through the tee peg.

When I play this shot, I set up with my hands more forward of the clubhead than normally. I keep a little more of weight towards my left foot on the backswing and try to take another divot on my throughswing. This helps me dig down and get under the ball. And finally I drive through the ball towards my target.

PLAYING A LONG APPROACH FROM A DIVOT

◆ ◆ ◆ ◆ ◆

When you are playing from a divot and need distance, do not think of using a 3- or 4-iron. In fact, avoid the long irons like the plague. Once again, the utility woods can come to your rescue, especially if you have the more modern type with a 'V-shaped' sole.

HOWEVER, IF the sole of your favourite wood is flat, that makes things more difficult. Imagine that shape of clubhead going into the divot. With a flat sole, you are going to hit behind the ball.

Modern fairway woods have a low centre of mass, especially the ones with loft. As a result, they can get the ball airborne quickly. You would not hit a 3-wood from a divot, and even a 5- would be ambitious, but the new 7- and 9-woods with 'V' soles are absolutely superb.

REALISTIC GOALS

But let's say you're 175 yards (160m) from the green and you do not have a utility wood. In that case, I would only feel comfortable recommending that you go down to about a 6- or 7-iron. Unfortunately, you will not get any more distance than usual because you will not get a flyer playing out of a divot. So

Digging yourself out of trouble

be realistic about what you can achieve. You may not be able to go for the green.

If there are also hazards around the green, such as bunkers, trees or water, being too ambitious could put you into further misery. The best move in that situation is to take a 9-iron or pitching wedge and just play the ball into position.

And remember, you must take a divot to play out of a divot!

Playing this shot requires commitment and belief. Make a compact backswing and drive through the ball with firm wrists and, most importantly, take another divot.

THE ETIQUETTE OF DIVOTS

The conventional wisdom has always been that players should replace divots. But now some golf clubs discourage this. Check the local rules on the scorecard, or talk to the secretary or pro to find out what their policy is. Golf clubs are finding that divots do not regrow well, and consequently that replacing them causes more of a problem than it solves. Increasingly, greenkeepers prefer to put seed and soil in the divot holes at night. So if you replace the divot, you may be just doubling their work. They will have to search the fairways to take them out, then fill the holes back in.

Aim left of the target as you are going to cut the ball out of this lie. You can do it!

TIGHT LIES AND HARDPAN
◆ ◆ ◆ ◆ ◆

Tight lies are often encountered on links and chalk-based golf courses, or others that do not have fairway irrigation systems — especially when the weather heats up. Because the fairways start to dry out and the grass does not grow lush — or is very fine and mowed closely — the ball will appear to be sitting down. Many golfers find this psychologically difficult. They are sure they will be unable to get under the ball and hit their normal shot.

IN FACT, on courses where the grass is lush, the ball does sit up slightly, with some air underneath. But that does not mean that golfers who are used to those conditions cannot hit off tighter lies.

For instance, the sub soil under many links courses is often much softer than it appears, and hitting down and through the ball, while taking a perfectly good divot, is fairly easy and straightforward — once the golfer gets used to the idea and is convinced that it is possible.

However, the tight lie that is truly difficult is the shot played off hardpan: dry patches that can bake into almost a rock-like hardness. But even this shot can be hit successfully, and with considerable backspin, if the proper set-up and swing are employed.

OVERCOMING FEARS

The biggest problem with playing from a tight lie is often simply in the player's mind. He or she is petrified of thinning or topping the ball. As a result, this golfer tries far too hard to get under the ball, which can lead to complete disaster.

When one tries to lift the ball on purpose, there is a tendency to stay back on the right foot, then swing upwards. Doing that will ensure topping or skulling the ball. Don't change your stroke for tight lies!

You should still go slightly down into the ball. However, if you are playing on clay or chalky soil — or any other type that has

become compacted in areas prone to wear — then I would add a note of caution. Hitting too hard down into that kind of surface could injure your wrists.

A ball lying on a tight lie or hardpan is most golfers' nightmare. But if you know how to play this shot, it's easier than it looks.

Keeping the weight on the front foot is the key to success in playing from a tight lie.

This is how *not* to play the shot. Trying to scoop the ball up into the air will lead to disaster.

Playing off hardpan

LANDING THE BALL SOFTLY

I always try to analyze my shots. If I have a very tight lie and I'm playing an approach shot from 50 or 60 yards (46 to 55m) to the green – needing to get up and over a bunker and land the ball softly – I want to be careful that I do not get any bounce.

So if I'm using a sand wedge, I set the ball back in my stance, then take that bounce away by closing the club down and putting my hands ahead of the ball. Going through the ball, I try not to dig in too much – which will be impossible anyway – and skim the surface, keeping my hands well ahead of the clubhead and my weight very much on the left foot.

Why? If the weight drifts back to the right foot, I will start to scoop at the ball.

HARDPAN

Hardpan is generally hard, dry, packed mud, and can be encountered anywhere on a golf course. Clay-based courses have the most hardpan, because as soon as it gets dry in the summer, the course starts to bake, the grass dies, and bare patches as hard as rock begin to form.

Hardpan can intimidate the average golfer, but you should keep in mind that you can make a good shot off the stuff. It's not impossible with the appropriate adjustments to your set-up, stance, and ball position.

VIOLENT CHECK

First, put the ball back in your stance – towards the centre or even nearer the right foot – and close the club face down slightly. On short approach shots, use a lofted club and hit down on the ball, trying your best to make a clean contact.

The fact is, you can actually get more backspin on this shot than a conventional one, because – if you think about it – you have nothing between the clubface and the ball.

And once you hit the ball, it will fly in quite low and bounce one, two or three times, then suddenly check quite violently – even spinning backwards from that point.

Here I'm playing a sand wedge off my back foot with a closed face. My hands are forward of the clubface throughout the stroke and my weight is planted firmly on my left foot. As I play the shot, I keep my hands and weight forward at all times.

PRO TIP

If playing off hardpan worries you and you are a short distance from the green, and the ground is very dry and hard, you might use a putter rather than a lofted club – if you can get away with it. Doing

this means you do not have to get under the ball and will give you added confidence. Or you might try using a 7-iron with a short putting or chipping stroke in an effort to get the ball running in. Even if you mis-hit this shot, it will not matter that much.

THE LONGER SHOT FROM HARDPAN

If you are playing from further away, do not make too many changes to your normal set-up and swing. I tend to put the ball farther back in my stance than usual and keep my weight fractionally more on my left foot. Reducing my usual weight shift will ensure I do not scoop the ball.

Again, be sure you play through the ball, thinking about making clean contact. You don't want to hit the ground behind the ball.

I recommend that you also look at the top of the ball – as I suggested you do with the fairway bunker shot – to ensure you get clean contact.

Above: Here I'm playing a shot off not only a very hard surface but my stance is also uneven. Therefore I'm limiting my weight transfer and concentrating on keeping my balance.

Above right and far right: I keep my backswing smooth in order to maintain balance and help strike the ball cleanly. A three-quarter backswing is plenty here and, as with my fairway bunker shot, I focus on the top of the golf ball.

Right: As I've swung through the ball, I've nipped it off the surface. This shot was played to a green some 100 yards (91m) away – when the ball landed it spun back some ten yards, which is not uncommon from this type of lie.

LOOSE LIES

◆ ◆ ◆ ◆ ◆

Loose lies are a particular problem on parkland and heathland courses in the autumn, when the ball can land on leaves, twigs or pine needles. But you can also get a loose lie in the rough on links courses and in the sandy areas around greens. Loose stones and soil are also a problem on many courses.

YOU SHOULD assess this shot carefully before hitting the ball, a precaution which many golfers fail to observe. Most players often tend to dismiss this type of lie as not very significant. Plunging in, he or she will give the ball a quick whack and hope for the best.

But if you look carefully at what you are confronted with on a loose lie, you'll see that there are several adjustments that should be made to hit this shot properly.

A clean contact from this lie is essential, so once again focus on the top of the ball.

ASSESS THE DEPTH

With a loose lie, the ball may actually be sitting off the ground, perched on leaves or other debris. If you merely hit downwards with an iron into this kind of lie, you may well leave the ball where it is as the clubhead skims harmlessly underneath, taking nothing but air with it.

So try to assess the depth of the lie, while at the same time remembering that if you disturb the ball, you will incur a penalty stroke. In addition, although you can remove loose debris from around the ball, you cannot rip out any plant, bramble or branch that is rooted in the soil or perhaps connected to a nearby tree or bush.

Another common loose lie is found when the ball lands on a bark pathway. First, you should assess how deep the material is. I would suggest taking up a stance, and, as in a bunker shot, wriggling your feet around to get a sense of how to balance yourself properly.

This is acceptable, as long as you do not start digging into the pathway, and especially near the ball, since it could move. By the way, always check the scorecard to see if you get a free drop off a bark pathway. That's certainly one way of coping successfully with a loose lie – but here are two other ways of playing a shot off a loose lie.

MAKING CONTACT

Getting clean contact with the ball is difficult off loose lies. I tend to use the same approach as a bunker shot, hitting an inch and a half (4cm) behind the ball to splash it out. Of course, you will not get any backspin, and the ball will run when it lands, so take that into account.

When the ball is sitting on twigs, using the splash shot becomes more problematic. If the debris is hard and brittle, it may well interfere with your strike and make any forward momentum difficult to achieve. Here you need to lift the club more abruptly, again using the out-to-in swing of a bunker shot, trying to pick the ball as cleanly as possible from the surface.

Be careful if removing debris around your ball not to move the ball, otherwise you'll be penalized. Only remove debris if you are certain it will not affect the lie of your ball – and remember that any vegetation moved must not be attached or living material.

Using a utility wood from a loose lie

If you're a long way from the green and distance is a requirement, use your 5- or 7-wood. This will have the added advantage of lifting the ball up over any obstacles in front of you.

Wedge it out

A wedge or 9-iron should easily be able to clip the ball out of a loose lie. Make a three-quarter swing and swing through the ball positively. Don't hit into the leaves and quit, otherwise you'll lose power.

HIT CLEAN

On parkland courses, you might find a loose lie along the tree line, where there are typically leaves, foliage and pine needles on the ground. Taking the distance from the green and the lie into consideration – let's assume you're about 120 to 130 yards (110 to 120m) away – I would suggest playing a 9-iron or wedge. Again, you want to lift the ball and hit it with some height, which means making clean contact, swinging from out-to-in in an attempt to fade the ball.

FOCUS ON TOP

One way to do this is by trying to hit the back of the ball first before the club makes contact with the ground. I focus on the top of the ball to make sure I hit it clean. Of course, you also run the risk of thinning or topping the ball, but I would prefer to do that rather than hit fat, or strike the ground before the ball, which deadens the shot and loses distance.

You might also consider using a utility wood if you can make any contact from a loose lie. The wood will help get the ball airborne, and the big soleplate will help glide the club across the surface, so it will not be as adversely affected by the lie.

With an iron, if anything gets between the clubface and the ball when playing off a loose lie, power will be reduced.

UPHILL LIES

◆ ◆ ◆ ◆ ◆

Playing off an uphill lie will make the ball fly higher, and thus travel a shorter distance, so you should always take at least one more club than normal (i.e. a 5-iron rather than a 6-iron). The other major effect this lie produces is a right-to-left movement of the ball, similar in effect to a draw.

PLAY THE ball further forward in your stance and position yourself in alignment with the slope, in this case allowing the right shoulder to drop down a bit more to mirror the rise in the land.

Weight distribution will also be affected. Don't fight the slope. Simply allow more weight to settle on to your back foot.

Now aim more to the right of the target because you are going to pull the ball slightly, and don't worry about your weight transfer, which will stay a little towards the back foot.

KEEPING BALANCE

One of the most important things to remember about any sloping lie is that you have to keep your balance throughout the swing. Take a few practice swings to determine how far back and through you want to bring the club in order to maintain good balance.

You might have to shorten your swing, thinking more in terms of an arms-and-hands shot, because you will not get as much body rotation and weight transfer as you would normally. If you did, you would simply fall over!

KEEPING FAITH

Because you will probably use more of a hands-and-arms swing for this shot – especially on the follow-through – the clubhead will tend to close. Aiming more to the right counteracts that.

Execute the shot with that in mind. You have to believe that the compensations that you have made will be enough to allow you to hit a reasonably good shot. Keeping faith with the shot is important.

You should also make sure that your rhythm is very smooth. Trying to force the shot is the worst sin you can commit. If you are afraid that you don't have enough club, take one more. And if you cannot do that, tell yourself that you must live with the consequences and keep it easy.

KNOW YOUR GAME

When playing from sloping lies, you have to think in the context of your own game, and apply that knowledge. For instance, if you tend to hit a slice or fade, you are not suddenly going to start to hit a draw from an uphill lie.

Instead, the slicer will hit a smaller slice, and a fader will hit the ball straight. But if you normally hit straight, you will hit with a draw. And if you hit it with a draw, you'll hit a hook.

It's all relative. So if you usually hit a fade, do not aim for a big draw, you will just hit it straight or fade it a bit.

Opposite: When you are confronted with an uphill lie, allow for the ball to move left with a draw (right-to-left) flight. So aim to the right, position the ball slightly further forward in your stance and angle your shoulders so that they follow the slope that your are playing from. Your weight will settle a little more towards your right foot.

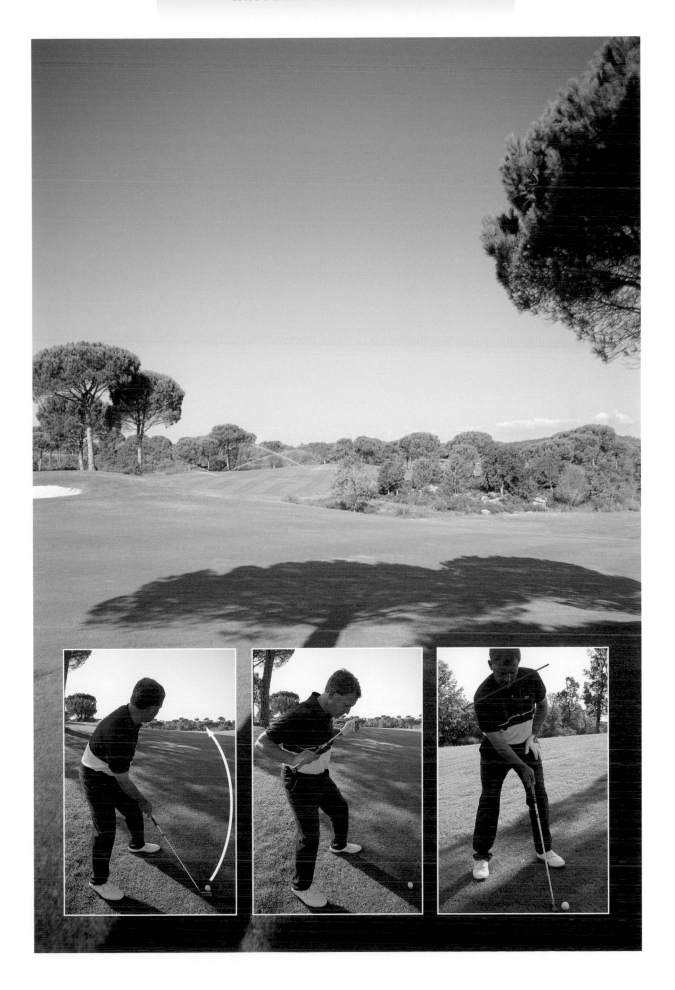

DOWNHILL LIES

◆ ◆ ◆ ◆ ◆

The downhill lie is generally a more awkward shot than the uphill lie for most players. It is always a little scary to have your back foot above your front foot, especially at the top of the backswing, where you may tend to lose balance.

HOW DO you compensate for the slope? The first thing to remember is that the lie will deloft the clubhead, which will mean that you will hit the ball lower and further than normal. So take at least one less club.

Then think about the effect on the spin imparted to the ball. From a downhill lie, you will generally hit the ball with a fade, or left-to-right. So aim more to the left and allow the ball to fade. Do not try to fight it.

FOLLOW THE SLOPE

In lining up, let your shoulders follow the line of the slope. Take an open stance, playing the ball further back because the club will come into contact with the ground sooner than on a level surface.

When you visualize the shot, remember that it will fly lower and have less backspin, so the ball will run further on its approach. Think about how it will land, kick and run on, and remember that it will work from left to right and kick in.

Picturing the shot always helps when playing from awkward lies. If you see a positive outcome and believe in the shot,

that will go a long way towards helping you to hit it properly. But many players allow themselves to be put off by the situation, and that is the beginning of the end. They will certainly not play the shot well because they will lack the mental confidence to do so.

FOCUS BACK

The downhill lie also poses more problems in terms of keeping your balance. You are definitely looking more at a three-quarter swing, with the weight tending to stay on your front foot when you take your backswing. You should accept that you will not get much weight transfer, which will shorten your swing anyway.

The follow-through will be fairly straightforward, but you must make sure you do not move ahead of the ball. It's easy to allow your head to drift too far forward when playing from this type of lie.

I try to ensure that I stay behind the golf ball by watching the back of the ball. Focus on the back of the ball. Otherwise, you'll top it. In addition, your rhythm needs to be very smooth. If you hurry the stroke, you will lose your balance.

The downhill lie is the most difficult for most players.

Place your ball further back in your stance.

PRO TIP

If you normally hit the ball with a draw, you will not suddenly hit a slice off a downhill lie – you might hit it straight. On the other hand, if you do slice or hit a fade, you might hit a massive slice from this type of lie. So take that into account.

Left: Angle your shoulders to match the slope.

Opposite: A three-quarter backswing with your weight staying more on your left foot is inevitable.

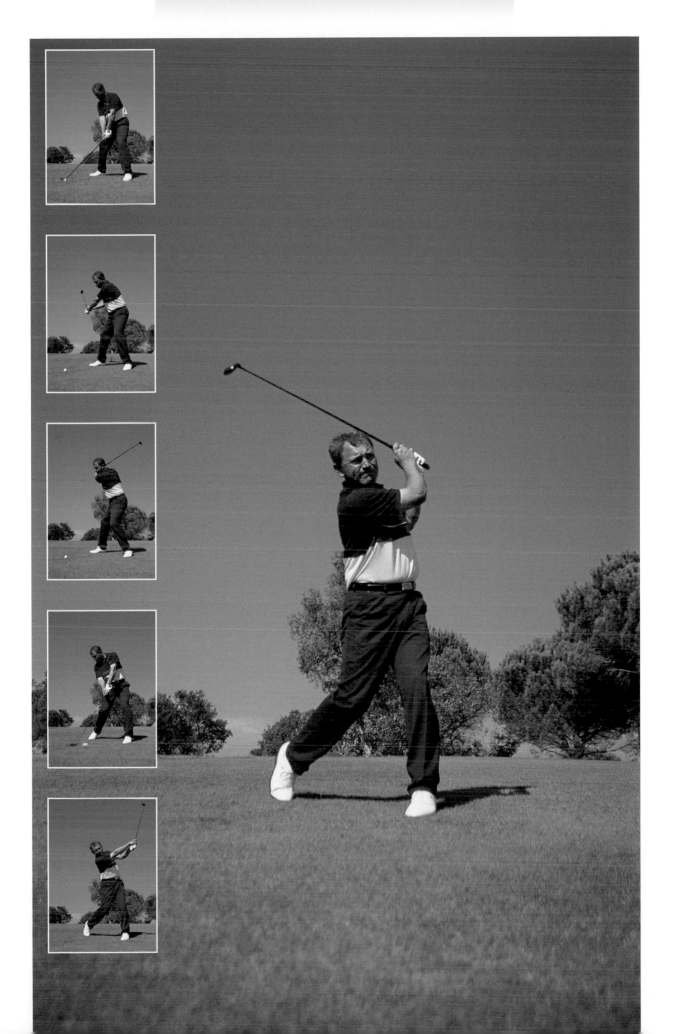

BALL ABOVE THE FEET

◆ ◆ ◆ ◆ ◆

Hitting a shot when the ball is above your feet is fairly straightforward, if you are aware of a few things. The ball will definitely move from right to left, or draw. You really cannot prevent that.

THE MORE acute the slope, the more the ball will move to the left from this type of lie. In fact, if you are playing from a really steep sidehill lie – with the ball perched right in front of your face – the ball will just go straight left.

AIM RIGHT

So you really have to aim right, and a long way off line, to hit the ball at your target, especially with a severe lie.

Grip down on the golf club. Depending on how far above your feet the ball is, you might have to grip a really long way down to reduce the club's length. With the worst of these lies, play a very lofted club, such as a sand wedge or a wedge, because the ball will go sideways, and the flight path could be very dramatic.

MORE CLUB

From a more conventional sidehill lie, with the ball maybe six inches (15cm) above your feet or less, the ball will still move to the left. So again, depending on the way you normally hit the ball, allow for that by aiming more to the right. Then grip down the golf club, which reduces its length and takes distance off the shot.

For example, if you have to grip three inches (8cm) down, that means hitting two or three more clubs than you would normally.

Above: Grip down the club in order to compensate for the slope and the fact that the ball is above your feet.

With the ball above your feet, aim more to the right of the target.

A more compact swing will ensure a good strike on the ball.

How to play the ball above your feet

A three-quarter back- and throughswing will help you to control this shot and hit the green with a controlled draw.

BALANCE IS THE KEY

When hitting off any sidehill lie, balance is the key component to your swing. So this is one instance where taking several practice swings – while observing proper etiquette and not

holding anyone up – is essential. Step back from the shot and find a position along the slope that is comparable to the place where your ball lies. Then take several practice swings, trying to keep your weight forward to compensate for the flat swing arc this lie forces you to use. Remember, if you lose your balance on this shot, you'll be defeated from the very start because you will fall backwards as you take the club away on the backswing. And if you do that, making any adjustment during the swing that allows a decent hit on the ball will be virtually impossible.

You judge that depending on the severity of the slope. If you don't grip down, you'll hit straight into the ground behind the ball.

TIGHT ACTION

If the ball is only slightly above your feet, don't change your normal golf swing. Just keep your tempo smooth and make a clean hit. You also do not need to change your ball position. Just allow for the ball to go further left than usual and play your normal shot.

But if the ball is six or eight inches (15 to 20cm) above your feet, then you have to go for a very precise strike. In this case, use a three-quarter swing, keeping your action nicely tight and compact, making sure you get clean contact with the ball.

Again, allow for the ball to go less distance because you have gripped down on the club. Don't try to overdo it, or get too much out of the shot.

The ball will draw more because you are standing more upright, which produces a flatter swing plane and causes the ball to move more right-to-left.

BALL BELOW THE FEET

◆◆◆◆◆

Playing a shot when the ball is below your feet is probably the most difficult shot for most golfers. With the ball so far down, we instinctively know that it's easy to lose our balance. So the first thing I think about when addressing the ball is keeping my weight back – or more towards my heels – and making sure it stays there.

O F COURSE, that does not mean that you do not get over the ball. When you take up your posture, you still must bend over sufficiently. But many players do not do this. They try to use their conventional posture. Standing up far too straight, they are surprised when they top the ball.

So, provide a counterbalance with your bottom. Stick it out. Sit back. Imagine you are almost sitting into the bank.

TAKE MORE CLUB

What effect will this lie have on the flight of the ball? It will definitely go left-to-right with a fade, and that could be significant. It could even produce a slice. Of course, that means a loss of distance, so you need to take more club to compensate. But taking more club will also help, since added length will lessen the effect of having the ball below your feet.

When you set-up, plant your weight firmly back on your heels, assume your posture close to the ball, then take a few practice swings. You have to feel comfortable with this shot, even though it's not a familiar one that you play everyday.

Sense what kind of swing will work, and how much weight transfer you will realistically get – until you almost fall over. Then try to get an idea of how to play well within that range.

STAY WITH THE SHOT

Do not use anything more than a three-quarter swing off a downhill lie, even if it isn't very severe – simply to ensure that you keep your balance. At the same time, make sure that you aim far enough to the left, and don't underdo it, because the ball will spin and definitely slice.

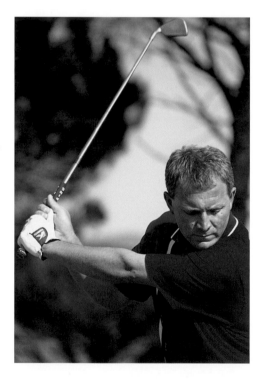

The ball below the feet is a difficult shot for any golfer. This key to success here is being realistic in deciding on the shot you are trying to play.

The key to success is to stay with this shot. That's the biggest failing of most players. You have to stay over the ball. If you come up even a fraction, it will be a disaster. You will top it.

Stay relaxed, stay over the ball, use a compact swing, and believe in what you are about to do, trusting that the ball will move from left-to-right. And remember to stay down as long as you can.

The ball below the feet

Left: At set-up concentrate on keeping your weight back towards your heels in order to maintain balance. Aim to the left as the ball will always fade or slice from this lie.

Left: At the top of the backswing there is just one thing that matters – balance.

Below left: At impact concentrate on watching the club strike the ball. It's essential that you stay down with this shot, otherwise you will top the ball.

PRO TIP

If you have problems that cause you either to top or to thin the ball, it's good practice to hit off downhill lies. With such a shot, you have to force yourself to stay with the ball. Most players do not find that very easy, so the more you practise this way, the more you will feel relaxed when you face one of these difficult shots on the course. Take some lessons on sidehill lies as well. Also, most driving ranges these days have mats with varying slopes. They allow you to play the full spectrum of shots whenever you practise.

Below: When you complete the swing, keep your balance and watch the ball fly left initially and then move right towards the target.

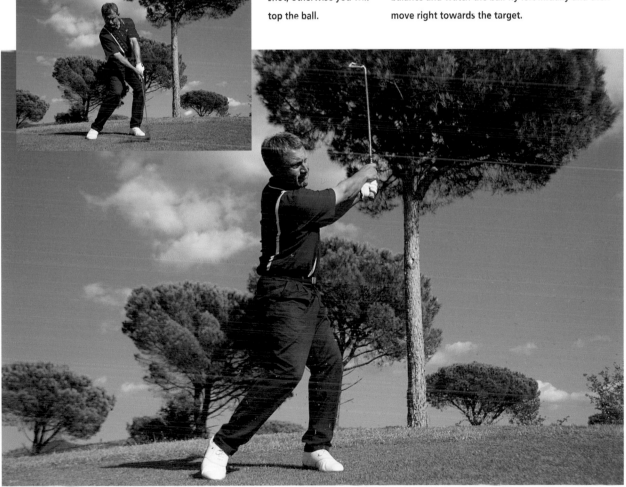

THE LOB FROM GREENSIDE ROUGH

◆◆◆◆◆

Leftie Phil Mickelson excels at hitting soft lobs around the green, even from the sort of horrific rough typically found at the US Open. And although Mickelson takes a longer backswing than I recommend for most players – because he has the clubface so far open – emulating his method will help you escape from greenside rough.

MICKELSON TRIES to get the ball as high as possible, to compensate for the lack of backspin caused by the high grass. Even with a lob in this situation, you have to accept that the ball will run a bit on landing. But if you were to play a more conventional chip from such rough, the ball would run forever.

LESS QUIT

Another reason to play a lob shot from greenside rough is because if you can really swing through it, you stand less chance of quitting on the ball. That's a big danger when playing out of this type of rough. The natural inclination is to let the club stay in the grass because your swing is inhibited.

If you hit the lob correctly, you will get some momentum on the clubhead as you come through, which produces the height as the loft on your wedge sends the ball up in the air.

Remember, it's easy for the clubface to snag and close in the rough. But with the clubface so open initially – or naturally lofted in the case of the lob wedge – that will help prevent turning the club over.

Using a lob wedge from greenside rough allows you to accelerate through the shot, reducing the possibility of your club getting caught up in the long grass.

Lob shot from rough

  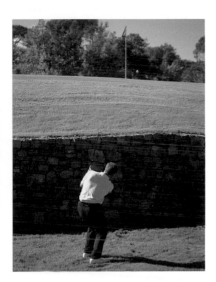

The only precaution when playing the lob wedge from the rough is that you have to take care not to pass clean under the ball without moving it forwards – most embarrassing!

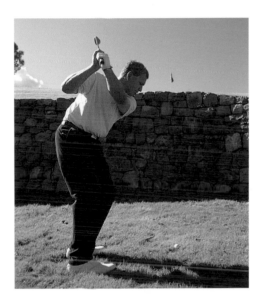

Below: A perfect use of the lob wedge.

PRO TIP

Even though you play a lob shot from greenside rough in a similar way to a bunker shot, be careful about hitting too far behind the ball. When I say you should play a splash shot, I am trying to emphasize technique, rather than the idea of hitting a few inches behind the ball. If the rough is deep enough, plenty of grass will inevitably come between the clubface and the ball, making contact slippery. Try to hit the ball as precisely as possible.

Lob from downhill rough lie

FAULTS AND CURES

◆◆◆◆◆

*Perfection in golf is
unattainable, but the best
players know how to correct
a fault quickly.*

CURING GRIP PROBLEMS

◆ ◆ ◆ ◆ ◆

Remember that the clubhead should open and close in synchronization with the rotation of the body during the swing. In the backswing, the clubhead is gradually opening, then closing until it is square at impact — before closing completely in the follow-through.

BUT WITH too much tension in the hands, the golfer prevents the clubhead from reacting naturally to the path of the swing. As a result, the clubhead stays open at impact, which is why the ball will veer off to the right.

FREE AGENTS

Holding the club too tightly may also cause more immediate problems in the backswing. When the swing is initiated with the hands – rather than a synchronized movement of the hands, arms and upper torso – a quick breakdown in the overall swing occurs. The upper body gets left behind, and the swing is destined to fail because it is no longer a co-ordinated movement.

What is the cure? It is essential that grip pressure remains light, so the wrists can

remain free agents and work in unison with the rest of the body in the golf swing – allowing the clubhead to flow correctly through impact with the ball.

Too much tension destroys that harmony.

FAULTY HANDS

After tension, the second major problem in the grip usually comes from the positioning of the hands on the club. The upper, or left hand, will often tend to creep around to the right, while the lower, or right hand, moves to the left. When that happens, the hands are working against one another, rather than as a solid unit.

Why does this occur? Most right-handed golfers unconsciously try to dominate and control the club with their right hand. The right forefinger and thumb can become

Above: If your hands are too far to the left on the club (bottom), a slice will be inevitable. The correct hand position is shown (top).

Left: When placing your hands on the club, ensure the back of your left hand and palm of your right hand are facing the target. This is the position to which they will naturally return.

Above: Place your hands lightly on the club. Nearly everyone who slices holds the club too tightly.

Right: A good grip enables you to swing back correctly.

Above: The strong or hooker's grip is certainly one to avoid.

especially influential in the player's stronger hand, working their way more and more over to the left.

Ben Hogan called the right thumb and forefinger the 'pincer' fingers. If they press in, all the tendons up to the top of the shoulder will tighten and even lock up, preventing a decent backswing. Additionally, the right arm will not fold properly as you go back, and the right arm will swing the club across the ball, producing a pull or slice.

CREEPING HANDS

At the same time, the left hand often tends to creep to the right, or go underneath, because it seems more comfortable in that position. As a rule I am less concerned with the left hand creeping under – into what is known as the traditionally strong grip – than I am with the right hand moving over.

The more the right hand comes around the club, the more that influences the positioning of both hands, and thus the way they present the clubhead to the ball at impact. This will also influence the positioning of the arms and shoulders in the set-up.

If the right hand gradually creeps around to the left, then the right shoulder becomes more and more dominant – the shoulder is actually pulled out of alignment. And the more the right shoulder moves out, the more likely the golfer is to swing from out-to-in.

Unfortunately, once again, this produces a slice or pull, a common fault among most golfers.

CLAP AND CLOSE

To overcome this tendency, try to assume a more 'natural' grip. Simply allow your arms and hands to hang down naturally, with the back of the left hand and the palm of the right hand facing the target – as if both hands were about to clap together, saluting your excellent grip position. Then just close the hands around the club.

Any other positioning of the hands will cause some degree of artificiality in the swing. You will have to manipulate your hands to get the clubhead back square at the point of impact.

Above: A weak or slicer's grip will cause you to swing across the ball and so cause it to pull or spin off to the right.

PRO TIP

Many top players now try to keep the right thumb and forefinger apart for fear of squeezing them together during the swing. This can tighten up the muscles of the arm and shoulder, so don't let that happen to you – it will overpower your swing. Instead, lay the thumb and forefinger on the shaft, but just leave them there, with a small gap between the two.

CURING ALIGNMENT PROBLEMS

◆ ◆ ◆ ◆ ◆

Proper alignment is crucial to developing a consistent golf swing. But, unfortunately, the average golfer often sets his or her body at the target, rather than aligning it parallel to the ball-to-target line.

WHY? IT is natural to associate lining up to a target in much the same way as one would aim and fire a rifle – which is down the shoulder line, bringing along the feet and hips.

This is totally wrong in golf!

When you swing a golf club, you are moving the clubhead at right angles to the ball-to-target line and the body must be parallel to that target line. Remember, it is the clubhead that hits the ball – not the body.

PULL AND SLICE

If you get in the way of your swing, you'll have a serious problem. With your body pointed directly at the target, it will be aligned too far to the right and you will be blocking the clubhead from swinging through to the target, and the resulting swingpath will be out-to-in. Generally, the golfer who commits the fault will pull their short irons and slice their longer clubs.

PRACTISE CORRECTLY

What is the cure for poor alignment? Practise with a purpose. When you go to the driving range, don't just set up in line with the edge of the mat or any other marker in your hitting area. Instead, pick a defined target and align yourself properly with that. Otherwise, you will probably set up incorrectly and start practising a fault, then ingrain a bad habit in your swing.

The best way to practise correct alignment is by putting some golf clubs on the ground to help you aim correctly. Place one club behind the golf ball, pointing straight to the target. Then put another one down just to the right of that and parallel to the target line.

Finally, place a third club parallel to the first two, but left of the ball – or nearer your feet. Now take away the club behind the ball and you are left with the proper alignment pattern indicated by the two parallel clubs.

To check your alignment – first place a club next to the ball pointing at your target, next place two clubs either side of the ball as shown below. Now you can check all aspects of your set-up starting with your clubhead and moving on to your body. Note any differences from the way you normally set up on the course and you've found your problem.

Your hips and shoulders need to be checked as well as your feet. They should all be running parallel to the ball-to-target line – that means that your body is pointing slightly left of your target, not at the target as most golfers believe.

Aiming the clubhead at right angles to both of the clubs on the ground, set your feet along the target line. Now you have a perfect set-up.

ON-COURSE ALIGNMENT CURES

Golf course architects are very clever. When they design a hole, they often make the tee box (teeing area) point right or left of the target, towards the rough or other problem areas. In such situations, you must remember to aim across the tee, which is difficult. Fairways can also be cut to tempt you off to the right or left of the hole.

The way to overcome such problems is relatively simple. Walk behind the ball and choose a target a few inches in front of the ball. Focus on a piece of grass, a divot, a twig or anything you can find that is along the correct ball-to-target line. The same goes for putting. You should always find something in front of the ball with which to line up.

BODY LAST

Now comes the most important part. The key to aligning properly is first to position the clubhead correctly along your chosen line, then set your body parallel to that line.

Don't ever do it the other way around! In other words, don't ever line your body up first. If you do that, your body will generally be misaligned.

Finally, on the course, if you are not playing in a competitive situation, you might try putting a club across your shoulders, hips or above your feet to check your alignment.

But in a practical sense, you cannot spend much time on such methods during a round. And, of course, any practice devices you might use on the range are strictly illegal on the golf course.

Use a short target in conjunction with the clubs you've laid down parallel to your ball-to-target line. This will show up any swing problems.

PRO TIP

Don't be embarrassed to practise proper alignment and aiming on the range. Golfers don't do that enough, and then they take their faults to the course. I've seen Jack Nicklaus practise many times, and, unless he is forced to do a very quick warm-up, he regularly puts clubs on the ground to promote proper alignment and practises with them in place through every club in the bag.

CURING PROBLEMS WITH BALL POSITION

◆ ◆ ◆ ◆ ◆

The position of the ball in your stance is also important to hitting good golf shots. If you put the ball in the wrong place relative to your set-up, you will make it difficult to achieve a decent strike.

WHEN THE ball is too far forward in your stance, or even in extreme circumstances outside your left foot, it ends up pulling your shoulders around because you have to reach for the ball. The right arm now becomes extremely dominant, which will lead to a variety of problems.

Quite often, the golfer who does not place the ball in the proper position will also have a bad grip and alignment. He or she may aim to the right, then put the ball miles too far forward in the stance.

COMMON NIGHTMARE

This can produce a nightmare scenario, though it is a common fault in many golfers. Now the player is so turned around that the feet are aiming to the right, and the shoulders are aiming to the left of the target line.

Given that set-up, there is no possible way to make a decent golf swing. The golfer will generally pull shots with the short clubs, and produce a big slice with the long clubs.

OPEN AND PUSH

Putting the ball too far back in the stance is much rarer, but it also causes numerous problems. Such a position will cause a push, or the ball flying straight to the right. Remember that body rotation in the swing

A ball placed too far forward in your stance will cause you to pull or slice the shot.

Far left: If your ball is too far forward, it will often lead to a closed club face and an out-to-in swingpath.

Left: A ball placed too far back in the stance will cause the club face to be open and an in-to-out swingpath.

Ball too far forward

opens and closes the clubhead, so if the ball is too far back, you will hit it too early in the swing, when the clubhead is still open.

Because the club is still coming in on an inside track, you might also impart unwanted spin to the ball. If the ball is not pushed off to the right, you might well send it off to the left with a hook spin.

The cure? In the previous section on alignment, I suggested putting two clubs on the ground that are parallel to the ball-to-target line when you practise. This should establish you in the proper set-up position. It's also an excellent way to check for proper ball position.

Put another club behind the ball, but perpendicular to the other two clubs. That

will tell you exactly where your ball is situated in your stance.

Practise this consistently, and you are halfway to achieving a proper ball position.

An out-to-in (slicer's) swing is the result of the ball being too far forward in the stance.

Below: If the ball is too far back in your stance, an in-to-out (hooker's) swing is likely.

PRO TIP

I do not mind if a golfer plays every shot off the left heel – which is what Jack Nicklaus advocates – as long as they are relaxed with that and can place the ball properly. On the other hand, the more traditional way of positioning the ball is also correct for many golfers, with the woods and long irons played off the left heel, the medium (5, 6 and 7) irons played midway between the centre and the left heel, and the short clubs (8, 9 and wedges) played from the middle of the stance.

It's very much an individual preference, and either choice is acceptable. I teach both, depending on which works better for each person. However, as with anything in golf, the key is to be consistent – and always to place the ball in the proper position relative to the clubhead and body along the target line.

Ball too far back

CURING POSTURE PROBLEMS

◆ ◆ ◆ ◆ ◆

Good posture is the cornerstone of an athletic golf swing.
The correct posture gives your swing balance, which will enable your
overall movement. But poor posture can interfere with balance, and then
everything can start to go wrong.

I BELIEVE YOUR body weight should be slightly backwards of centre, towards the heels of your feet. If a golfer's weight moves forward of centre, an out-to-in swingpath will result causing the club to cut across the ball. When your weight moves forwards, your upper body will generally begin to sway forwards as well.

If this happens, the golfer is putting his or her body in the way of the swing, especially as he or she comes through the ball. The golfer is then forced to move the club farther outside the normal swingpath – or farther away from the body – hitting across the ball with a glancing blow that starts it spinning. The common result is a slice to the far right of the target with the longer clubs, and a pull with the short clubs.

SWING AROUND

One way to maintain good posture and balance is to keep your weight slightly back of centre. Throughout the movement of the swing, you want to rotate around the pivotal points of the right heel on the backswing, and the left heel on the throughswing.

While doing this, you must keep the body exactly the same distance from the ball at all times. Only then can you allow the club to swing truly around you.

If you move the body either closer to the ball – or farther away from it – you will experience a loss of balance, which will upset everything in the swing. The golfer is then in a different position at impact from that at address, and the swing can never be consistent.

Indeed, you will be struggling to rebuild your movement while trying to swing the club correctly.

SWING PLANE

Another way to focus on posture and balance is to think about swing plane. If the upper body's position lifts during the

Most posture problems are caused by trying to get too close to the ball. Be bold, stand tall, bend from the hips and sit back – it's simple.

The athletic posture

The 'head up' position

backswing, it creates a swing plane that is too flat. And when the upper body drops dramatically, it sets up too high a swing plane, with the arms lifting in the air, independently of the body.

Remember that swing plane is formed by the initial posture at set-up, and that the angle of the spine dictates the plane. We want the spine to stay in one place throughout the swing, and if that angle remains constant, then the club can move around the body on a consistent circle.

But if the spine moves up or down, it will take the arms, hands and club with it, dramatically altering the swing plane and thus the golf shot.

MIRROR CURE

How do you cure posture faults? One way is by using a mirror. Check your posture in this way as often as you can, examining your spinal angle from behind. Better still, capture yourself using a video camera, or get a friend or golf pro to take a look regularly. While practising this, close your eyes and try to ingrain the feeling of correct posture in your mind.

How do you know what the ideal posture is for you? That's dictated by your height and the length of your arms and clubs. The shorter player will be more upright, the taller one more bent over.

Here's how to take up your particular posture correctly:

1. Using a golf club, bend your upper body forwards from your hips – not from your waist – keeping the head high and the chin nicely clear of the chest. Try to retain the integrity of your head position vis-à-vis a reasonably straight line down to the base of your spine. When you bend forwards over the ball, you must retain that line – that's your spine angle.

2. Now let the clubhead touch the ground.

3. Your weight will be somewhat forward, so you'll need to counterbalance that by sticking your bottom out. Adding a little flex to the knees will help to push your bottom out until you feel you're almost leaning against the back of a chair.

Exactly how the above moves are accomplished will vary somewhat with every player, and with every club that is used.

A very tall golfer with a short club will have to stick his or her bottom out quite a bit – because otherwise too much weight will remain forward. On the other hand, a shorter person with a long club will scarcely need to bend over at all, or consequently stick their rear out very far.

Above: If you struggle with your head being too low at set-up – practise keeping your head up as you bend forwards.

If your legs are too straight, you will have to bend forwards excessively.

Too much flex in your legs and you will be too erect in your upper body causing a top shot.

CURING THE SLICE

♦♦♦♦♦

In order to cure the slice, you have to start with the set-up. Check your grip, alignment, ball position and posture. If the set-up is wrong, you cannot fix your golf swing. Generally, the swing itself is the last thing that is wrong.

BUT ASSUMING you have a perfect set-up, what other factors can we look at?

One is the swingpath through the ball. That will be very influential. If you are slicing, you are swinging across the ball from out-to-in, imparting sideways – or clockwise – spin to the golf ball.

DO THE OPPOSITE

What's the cure? Once you are reasonably sure your set-up is correct, try to do the opposite of what is causing the problem. In other words, you should try to swing along an in-to-out swingpath and make sure you are freely releasing the club.

Try only halfswings at first, in an attempt to gain a feel for that movement and establish it as your swingpath. Remember, if you are slicing, you have become used to swinging from out-to-in, and often you will not even realize you're doing it.

DEFINED TARGET

Then pick a defined target on the golf range, place some clubs on the ground to ensure your alignment is correct, and try to make the ball move from right to left. In other words, you must literally try to draw the ball.

As slicing is caused by swinging the club to the left of the target, practise swinging the club more to the right of the target.

It's the one I've seen so often – the out-to-in swingpath can only cause a pull or slice.

Bad swing

Out-to-in swingpath

PRO TIP

Hit some shots from a sidehill lie, with the ball several inches above your feet. This can help you to produce a better swing plane and promotes an in-to-out swingpath.

Above: The out-to-in swingpath illustrated in detail.

Below left: Ensure your hands are lightly placed on the grip.

Below: Check your ball position is not too far forward in the stance.

In addition, make sure your hands are light on the grip so your wrists are free and the clubhead can release. Holding too tightly helps create a slice.

Below: Here I demonstrate the correct swing. Note the differences at set-up, top of backswing and through the ball.

Good swing

CURING THE HOOK

◆◆◆◆◆

The hook is often the result of any number of set-up problems. Generally, the hands have crept too much to the right, a position which is known as a strong, or hooker's, grip. And as the hands creep round, the shoulders tend to get more and more closed, until they are aiming too much to the right.

WHEN THESE faults occur, the golfer might also begin to position the ball too far to the back of his or her stance.

In this situation, it's also common for the golfer inadvertently to open the clubface far too much. Why? As the ball begins to move more and more right-to-left, the golfer becomes petrified of the left-hand side of the golf course, and will do anything to stay right. So, they tend to open the clubface, aiming to the right of the target line.

Of course, most golfers do not realize the clubface is opening. In fact, they would bet their life they're aiming straight, when they are actually aiming as much as 30 degrees right. Now the ball can only go right and the swingpath gets increasingly in-to-out, aggravating the tendency to hit a hook.

TROUBLE ZONE

But if the golfer swings in-to-out and hits the ball with the clubface square, the ball will start spinning right to left. Now the ball will start straight, and then begin to veer off to the left. By contrast, if the ball is hit with the clubface even only slightly closed – say one or two degrees – that will produce a duck-hook, or snap-hook.

In this case the ball hardly gets airborne, flying very low and rapidly curling left. As Lee Trevino says, you can talk to a fade, but you can't talk to a hook, because once the ball starts spinning low and left, it will bounce violently and spin off into trouble when it hits the ground.

INITIAL FLIGHT

What is the cure? Look at your set-up first, examining the grip, alignment and ball position. Then check the clubface. If it's wide open, square it up behind the ball. Finally, put some clubs on the ground to check your alignment and pick a defined target, working on the initial line of flight of the ball.

If you can get a friend to stand behind you at this point, that will be helpful. He or she can tell you if the ball is starting right, and spinning, which you will not be able to see yourself.

Using the clubs for proper alignment, work on starting the backswing in a straight line, trying to get some initial width. Then as

CHECK THE LINE OF YOUR DIVOT

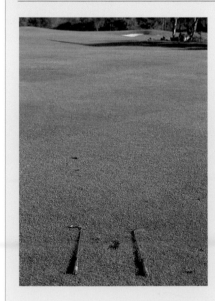

One of the telltale signs of an excessively in-to-out golf swing will be shown in the divot you take. Look carefully at your divot after you've hit your shot. If it's pointing to the right of the target you're swinging too much in-to-out, thus causing the hook shot.

The hooker will generally aim too far right (in an attempt to compensate for the ball going left) and then produce a flat swing with excessive hand action.

you come through the ball, think about pulling the club through with your left arm, keeping the left arm and hand ahead of the clubhead, swinging out-to-in in a way rather like hitting a bunker shot.

You are literally trying to cut the ball, or move it from left to right, trying to hit a slice.

ON AND OFF

Fuzzy Zoeller once said that he had the easiest job in the world striving to be a good golfer because he only suffered from one fault, and that was hooking the ball. So what he tries to do on any shot is to slice it.

But as with all hookers, they may be on form one day, and off the other. The American big-hitter John Daly is another classic example. He is long and extremely powerful, but tends to hook the ball. On a course such as St. Andrews – where he won the British Open a few years ago – he is relatively all right, because there's little trouble on the left. But put him on a course with danger on the left, and he has a serious problem.

As with curing the slice, you have to attempt the opposite shot to fix a hook. Try to visualize slicing the ball. Try to start the ball to the left of the target and make it spin to the right. That's the quickest way to cure a hook.

Left: Once again check your body alignment – so often this is the root of the problem.

Below: A great cure for the hook: give control to your left arm and try to cut across the ball as though you are trying to fade or slice.

CURING THE SHANK

♦ ♦ ♦ ♦ ♦

Is there a more dreaded word in golf? I will not even repeat it, except to say that this sometimes contagious 'mis-hit' happens when we strike the ball with the hosel of the club, or the spot where the shaft joins the clubface. The ball will then careen off wildly, usually at right angles to the target line.

THE CAUSE can often be attributed to the player standing too close to the ball, or shifting his or her weight too far forwards. But most of the time, the 'shank' (there, I said it!) is caused by tension.

The arms and hands lock up and the body takes over, with the shoulders pushing the clubhead down the wrong swingpath.

SHARPER STRIKES

The cure for this fault is to practise sharper strikes with your feet close together. This exercise restores timing and promotes better feel for weight transfer and the free swinging of the hands and arms.

And lastly, take a deep breath to make sure your breathing is relaxed and steady, and then lighten your grip pressure.

The shank is when the ball is struck in the heel of the golf club and is often caused by standing too close to the golf ball.

Practise half swings

Left: An instant
cure – address the
ball on the toe of
the club.

Above left: The most common
cause of shanking is too much
tension, a head-down position
at address and being too close
to the ball.

Above: If you get rid of
the tension at set-up,
you'll almost always
cure your shanking.

Practising half shots is a great way to
get rid of shanking and sharpen your
strike on the golf ball. Keep your hands
light and allow the club to swing freely –
enjoy yourself and things will improve.

CURING THINNED AND TOPPED SHOTS

◆ ◆ ◆ ◆ ◆

Thinning, or topping, the ball can be caused by a number of factors, but the most common one I see among golfers is their tendency to keep the head rigidly down during the swing, preventing proper body rotation.

WHY IS that? The average golfer often strives to look squarely at the ball. But remember, you don't have to stare at the ball with both eyes forever! For the most part, you only see the ball out of one eye as you take the club back, and keep watching the ball until until you strike it.

FREEZING UP

But many golfers are so keen to stare the ball down – while making sure their head does not move – that they freeze. Then, when they do try to swing back, the head does not rotate as it should, and the upper body is prevented from opening up, or making a full turn.

This will often lead to a second error, especially if the idea that 'you must keep your eye on the ball' and 'keep your head down' is constantly moving on a loop through your brain. Because your head has not rotated properly, and your initial move has not been correct, you will now inadvertently force yourself to move your body down towards the ball – which is a disaster.

BREAKDOWN

This produces a drop in the spine angle, and from there, you cannot hope to rotate the body correctly behind the ball. The arms will also break down, and you will lose width in your swing. In addition, because you are now closer to the ball, your balance will also be severely affected, since your weight is probably too far forwards.

Now you have a tenth of a second from the top of the backswing until you hit the ball, and yet you are three or four inches (8

GETTING OFF THE GROUND

Concentrate on grooving your swing and transferring your weight correctly to avoid thinning or topping the ball. Put a tee peg in the ground and take half-swings, gently sweeping the tee out of the turf to ingrain the idea of a correct swingpath and hitting through the ball in a way that lets the loft of the clubface do its job properly. Now replace the tee with a ball and resist the temptation to try scooping the ball off the ground. Secondly, focus on the idea of moving your weight back, then forward, by swinging slowly, concentrating on how your weight shifts back to the right foot, then forward around your left (see picture right). If your weight shift is timed correctly, and fully executed, the clubface will simply brush the ball off the turf, striking it at the centre – rather than on the upper half (see picture above).

Bad form resulting in topped or thinned shot

Ironically the topped shot is often the result of trying too hard to keep your head down or rigidly still.

A good swing to prevent topping

A fluid swing starting from a good posture and position will rarely cause you to top the ball. And rather than telling yourself to keep your 'head down', simply tell yourself to 'watch the clubhead strike the ball'. This will result in less intensity and thus no restrictions in your movement.

to 10cm) closer to the ball than you should be, or were at address. What are you going to do? You have to come up. As you swing through, you have to lift your body to get decent contact with the ball. But that is very difficult, and at that point, you are generally destined to do one of two things:

1. You will lift up too much to compensate, and thus you will top or thin the ball – also known as skulling it.
2. Or you will not lift up enough, and you will hit the ground way behind the ball – what we call hitting it fat.

MIRACULOUS MISHAP

But what will your friends say when you ask for advice? They'll say you lifted your head, and that maybe your left arm is breaking down!

So on the next shot, you'll try even harder to stay down, which makes you drop even lower and further increases your difficulty. Once again, your body will not turn correctly, you will lose all the width in your swing, and even if you manage miraculously somehow to hit the ball – it will be without any power.

FULL TURN

The way to cure this fault is to allow your head to rotate naturally behind the ball and to complete a full turn by not fixing your gaze on the golf ball with both eyes. At first, you may feel as if you are swaying off the ball, but if you transfer your weight properly and keep your spine angle intact, you cannot help but make a decent backswing.

Practise this motion in a mirror to convince yourself.

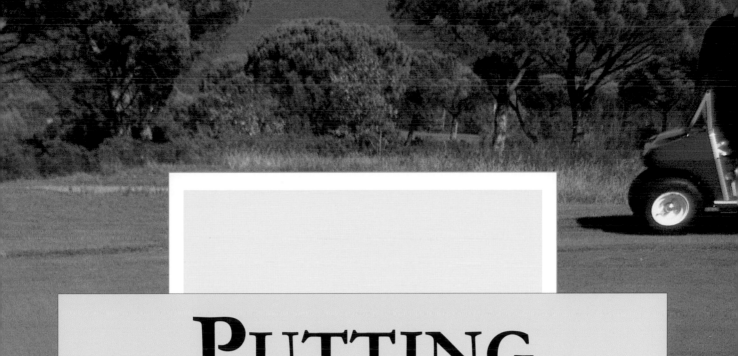

PUTTING MASTERCLASS

◆◆◆◆◆

*Putting accounts for at least
50 per cent of the game.
So start working towards
cutting your score dramatically
by more effective putting.*

READING THE GREEN

◆ ◆ ◆ ◆ ◆

From the moment I hit a shot into the green, I start to size up how I shall go about sinking the putt. As I walk up the fairway, I try to judge the surrounding land to get an idea of the slope and the general lie of the land.

IS THE green on flat land, or part of a ridge that falls away from a hill? Is there water nearby, and do the natural contours lead in that direction? If it were raining heavily, which way do I think the land would drain?

Once I get closer, I start to analyze the slopes on the green itself, plus the colour and coarseness of the grass to gauge the speed of the green. On hot summer days, or in warmer climates, I might even consider the time of day to give me a clue about that speed. The later it is in the afternoon, given such conditions, the longer the grass and possibly heavier the air will be, which will slow a putt down.

Finally, unless I'm putting first, I spend any free time I have practising my stroke. Then I watch how others hit their putts. If I can, I also walk around as much of the green as possible – without causing any delay to my partners or the golfers behind us – getting more of a feel for the texture and grade of the putting surface.

COMBINING FACTORS

Of course, everything I have just described constitutes a method for judging the speed, slope and run of the green I'm about to play – information vital to making my putt.

Those are the three key words in learning how to read greens, and becoming a good putter – speed, slope and run.

PICTURE GALLERY

As I've stressed about every aspect of the short game, before you can hope to lower your scores significantly, you have to put in the time on the practice range. This is certainly true of putting above all else.

By the time that you reach any green during play, you should have logged countless hours hitting putts uphill and down, along left-to-right breaks or vice-versa, and on slow, fast, wet or windy surfaces.

That way, once you take the first look at your putt in any circumstance, you'll have some experience to fall back on. You will have compiled that mental picture gallery that is necessary in order to judge your putt – although that's only half the battle. Here's how to handle the other half.

Reading a green is an art in itself. But there can be no doubt that if you can read the slopes on a green, you will hole many more putts. If you can visualize how water would flow on a slope, that's how the ball will roll too.

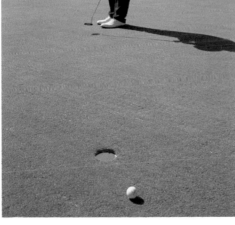

Above left: Visualize the roll of the ball before playing the shot.

Left: Always aim to get the ball past the hole – don't leave it short.

Above: With long putts speed is so important – try to get the ball inside a 3ft (1m) circle around the hole.

FIRST GLANCE

How much will your putt break? If at all.

All three factors – speed, slope and run – could come into play here, so start by squatting behind your ball and taking a visual cue. You can also walk to the hole and try to visualize the line from there back to the ball. Returning from the hole to the ball will also help you to get a sense of what lies between, not to mention allowing you to pause to look at the putt from the side.

USING VISUAL AIDS TO LINE UP A PUTT

What are the professionals doing when they mark their ball, crouch down, and then seem to fiddle with the ball before placing it back on the green? Many times, they're trying to line up the manufacturer's name with the target line to the hole. This visual aid can help both in aiming your putter blade correctly and instilling confidence, since you are giving yourself a specific cue that's easy to focus upon. Just imagine the ball rolling end over end – with the manufacturer's name holding steady at the equator – down the line to the hole. Another way of using the maker's name is to place it at the back of the ball, where the putter blade will strike first. Again, this gives you something to aim at and a way of concentrating on bringing the putter into the ball cleanly, before sweeping it away. It's easy to let your concentration drift when putting, especially if you lack confidence on the greens. Using either of these methods will get you into a sharper frame of mind and thinking about a positive result.

Once you have a sense of how far the ball will break, overplay that break. One of the most common errors I see is golfers who underread breaks. At least if you overread the break, you still have a chance to get the ball in the hole, since you will be coming in from the high side of the hole, rather than the low one – where you have no chance.

What do I mean by this? Consider a putt that breaks from right-to-left. That means the slope rises from left to right, or falls from right to left, depending on how you wish to view it. Thus, overestimating the break will probably put you above the hole when the putt starts to die, with a chance that the ball can still fall into the cup.

Underhit this putt and you end up below the hole falling away down the slope.

LAST TURN

Next, consider the speed. The ball will break more on fast greens than slow ones, because there is less friction to slow it down. So play more break on a fast green, and watch how the ball starts to curve more as it dies near the hole. Of course, if you are putting downhill, there will be even more speed and break.

In the above example, you should always try to hit the ball past the hole, even if that prospect frightens the life out of you. Above all, don't be so tentative that you freeze up and stab at your stroke. And don't try to finesse this type of putt, hoping it will die into the cup on the last roll. Even if you run well past the hole, you'll at least have a simpler uphill putt coming back.

DISTANCE DICTATES

When playing uphill putts, you must tell yourself to hit the ball harder. That is often quite difficult, and is rather similar to going from playing on fast greens to slow ones. Often, some mental or physical inhibition just will not let us loosen up in these situations, and some golfers consistently leave such putts short.

So again, try to visualize hitting the ball past the hole, or charging it. Of course, by that I do not mean hammering the ball.

Always putt with a smooth, rhythmic stroke, letting the length of the putt dictate the distance the ball travels.

I find that the best way to overcome this problem is to concentrate on my follow-through. Think about stroking the putter fluidly toward the hole and the rest will fall into place.

COLOURFUL CLUE

Finally, consider the grain, or the direction in which the grass lies on the green. The longer and thicker it is, the more it will affect your putt.

How does grain affect your play? A putt hit downgrain will run faster and farther than one hit upgrain. And if the grain runs across the line of your putt, the ball will break more in the direction the grain is running, and less so the other way.

You can tell which way the grain is running by its colour. If it looks light or has a sheen, you are looking down the grain, as opposed to upgrain, where the grass will appear more dark and coarse.

Another way to determine the grain is to examine a golf hole. If one edge looks slightly frayed – what you're seeing is the actual ends of the grass projecting over the hole – that's the way the grain is running.

The colour of the grass will help you to decide how the ball will run. A shiny light colour will indicate you're putting down the grain – a quick putt. A darker colour signifies that you're putting against the grain – a slower putt.

If you're playing early in the morning, you will often see dew on the grass. If others have preceded you, they will have created marks that clearly show how the ball will move across the green. This can be very useful in judging your putt, but remember that the dew will slow the ball dramatically as the putt loses speed – so be bold with your stroke.

THE MENTAL SIDE

◆ ◆ ◆ ◆ ◆

Now that you know how to execute the basic putting stroke, and how to judge distance and break, let me address the idea of confidence. I believe that the art of building faith in your putting stroke starts on the practice green, and that even if you only have a few minutes to spare before teeing off for a round, this is the place where you should spend that time.

START BY hitting only short putts of under three feet (1m) – in other words, the sort that once on the course you might consider 'gimmes', and that might even be conceded to you by your playing partners.

But how many times have you seen other golfers – or even found yourself – standing over such short putts and losing it? The knees turn to jelly, the arms and hands start twitching, and pretty soon a putt has been missed that most people could normally make in their sleep. From that point on, your entire round may go south.

Believe me, it happens to the best of us.

POSITIVE SOUNDS

So confine yourself to positive action before each round. Hit at least a dozen short putts, striking each ball firmly and with conviction, using your basic stroke, and listening for the sound of the ball striking the metal pin in the hole, or rattling into the cup.

Now you can head for the course feeling decisive, the memory of each sweet, well-struck putt carrying over to your game.

TRUST YOURSELF

Once on the course, trust yourself. Here is where the hours of practice, the experience, and your natural instincts should take over.

Far left: Even if you only have a few minutes before a round, use the time constructively by hitting some short putts and building confidence for your round.

Left: This is one of the many exercises I use and teach – start close to the hole, knock the putt in, and then move back to the next ball. Continue until you have holed all the balls.

Above: See the putt in your mind – and then feel it in your arms and hands.

Remember, the first glance you take at the line of a putt should tell you almost everything you need to know about the shot, and be enough to let you proceed to play it.

You aren't building a bridge. You don't need a calculator to figure the angles. This isn't rocket science. Feel the putt into the hole.

POSITIVE IMAGES

You can also try conjuring up a positive picture to help you prepare for the shot.

Relax and imagine the ball rolling down the line, then plopping into the cup. Visualizing a successful putt is halfway to making that putt. On the other hand, letting negative thoughts intrude into your mind will almost guarantee you miss the putt. And the next one.

But remember, if you have played even one really decent round in your life, you know you can sink a lot of putts. You know you're capable of making more putts than you miss.

So go ahead. Trust your ability and strike the ball.

Above: Learning to trust your stroke is the most important part of putting.

EQUIPPED WITH CONFIDENCE

Having confidence in your equipment is a sure way to instill more confidence when putting. If your putter has a flattened grip on the front side, have it checked frequently by a qualified PGA pro or clubmaker to ensure the grip is precisely angled at 90 degrees to the face of the putter blade. Any minor discrepancy here can seriously affect your alignment and lead to consistently missed putts, though you are not likely to know the reason – and thus will start blaming your own technique. If that happens, you might eventually lose confidence in your abilities and miss too many easy putts during a relaxed round, and bunches under competitive pressure. So have the grip examined – and if need be re-aligned – on a frequent basis. Then you will approach each putt with at least one more positive in your bag.

INDEX

◆ ◆ ◆ ◆